Helen Wright was the founder and the first head coach of the University of Alberta's Pandas rugby team. She was a pioneer in establishing women's rugby as a provincial, national, and international sport – defying stereotypes at a time when the sport was dominated by men – primarily through leading by example as a player, coach, and administrator. Rugby's inclusiveness, related to both ability levels and physical diversity of players, was the key factor in Wright's commitment and advocacy for the sport.

Raised in Williams Lake, B.C., Wright came to Edmonton to study psychology at the University of Alberta. She was introduced to rugby as a spectator in 1977 and started playing in the position of "hooker". Wright represented Alberta from 1986–1988, and she participated in the first Rugby Canada women's national team game against the USA in Victoria in November 1987.

Wright served as managing director of the Alberta Rugby Union from 1987–2001, exerting significant influence over the continuing development of youth and women's rugby in the province.

Wright led the Pandas for five seasons – 1999 to 2003 – and secured five successive national championships. She coached the Rugby Canada U23 Women in 2005 when they defeated the USA in two test matches.

Her formal coaching qualifications included Level 1 and 2 International Rugby Board Coach Trainer, Levels 1, 2, and 3 of the National Coaching Certification Program. Wright became the CIS Coaches Association President (Rugby) and oversaw the preparation of the documentation to keep women's rugby and include men's rugby in the CIS (Canadian Intervarsity Sport).

Helen Wright's involvement with rugby extended far and wide, including being the only female coach to coach a Men's First Division team in the Alberta Cup.

Her extraordinary success as a player, coach, and administrator in rugby at the U of A and far beyond, is a tribute to her unstoppable passion and commitment to push boundaries.

This book is dedicated to my family; Gary, my husband who encouraged and pushed me to "tell my story". My children, Amanda and Sean, who journeyed right along beside me through the whole time. It is also dedicated to all those coaches who have contributed to the lives of their players and students; especially my dear friends: Amelia, Kerry, Maxi, Matt, and Sluggo.

Helen Wright

BAREFOOT FLYING

AUSTIN MACAULEY PUBLISHERS™
LONDON • CAMBRIDGE • NEW YORK • SHARJAH

Copyright © Helen Wright 2021

All rights reserved. No part of this publication may be reproduced, distributed, or transmitted in any form or by any means, including photocopying, recording, or other electronic or mechanical methods, without the prior written permission of the publisher, except in the case of brief quotations embodied in critical reviews and certain other noncommercial uses permitted by copyright law. For permission requests, write to the publisher.

Any person who commits any unauthorized act in relation to this publication may be liable to criminal prosecution and civil claims for damages.

All of the events in this memoir are true to the best of author's memory. The views expressed in this memoir are solely those of the author.

Ordering Information
Quantity sales: Special discounts are available on quantity purchases by corporations, associations, and others. For details, contact the publisher at the address below.

Publisher's Cataloging-in-Publication data
Wright, Helen
Barefoot Flying

ISBN 9781647506919 (Paperback)
ISBN 9781647506926 (ePub e-book)

Library of Congress Control Number: 2021918984

www.austinmacauley.com/us

First Published 2021
Austin Macauley Publishers LLC
40 Wall Street, 33rd Floor, Suite 3302
New York, NY 10005
USA

mail-usa@austinmacauley.com
+1 (646) 5125767

Table of Contents

Prologue	11
Rugby Terms	16
Lexicon	19
Chapter 1	21
In the Beginning (September 1955–September 1970)	
Chapter 2	46
From Player to Coach (1977–1988)	
Chapter 3	62
The Job (1988–2000)	
Chapter 4	75
And No One Says a Word (1990–1995)	
Chapter 5	91
Becoming Part of the Clan	
Chapter 6	100
It Isn't About the Outcome, It's About the Performance (1989–2004)	

Chapter 7   120

There Is No "I" In Team

Chapter 8   135

Playing the Nanapoopoo Game

Chapter 9   146

Fear, The Big Inhibitor

Chapter 10   158

Barefoot Flying

Chapter 11   167

Hope and Humor What We All Need

Chapter 12   177

The Closing

Prologue

When I was a child and before I learned about the limitations of life, coaching, and the world, I experienced the joy of physical movement. There was a field near my house where the calves would nibble the clover down to a soft emerald carpet. I would run across the soft, wet field in my bare feet. I was weightless, powered by the sheer joy of movement and unencumbered with any knowledge of limitations. My body moved naturally, intuitively, without any thought. My sole purpose was to feel and enjoy this physical form. My spirit was free. At that moment, I believed I could fly. I later referred to that sensation as "barefoot flying."

I was young and still unaffected by the surrounding world and the limiting view of what we as humans have the capacity to do. Throughout time, people have created the plethora of rules and regulations about who you can be and what you can do. These rules are guided by cultures, religions, science and the ever-present human desire to 'succeed,' to 'win.' It has taken me a lifetime to come full circle to realize that the original desire to feel joy is really the only reason I am here.

I did experience the sensation of "barefoot flying" again later in my life. I was surprised to find it on a rugby field, simply playing with other athletes. We played spontaneously, allowing intuition to guide our actions and fueled again by the joy resulting from this freedom of movement and spirit. This time, the sensation was heightened by a magical feeling of connectedness and shared joy.

My journey through coaching and life has led me to realize that through all of the twists and turns along the path, I was inadvertently always searching for that same sensation of joy. Though I may not have recognized it at the time, as a coach, I was seeking to provide that type of experience for the athletes. I was trying to show them a piece of who and what they could be, regardless of what anyone had told them before. As a person, I was learning that the joy I had experienced as a free-spirited child—a child who knew no limits—was available to me as a coach as well. The source of this joy is not external. This joy does not result from winning. I learned that we all carry this joy within us. I learned that to access this joy, we need only remember who we are and allow ourselves the freedom to fly. Just as we did as children, when we were "barefoot flying."

This book is the story of my professional and personal journey as one of the first female coaches in the sport of rugby.

When I first thought of writing this story, I spent many agonizing moments questioning my authority to tell the world my vision of how sport could change the world one player at a time. I had a combination of my own and the world's ego echoing in my ears about the fact that I didn't have any celebrity, earth-shattering success story to validate anything that I was spouting. All my "not good enough" issues were firmly entrenched and delivering the same amount of self-doubt that had plagued me most of my coaching career.

I have been the most fortunate person to have access to a sacred place in the Rocky Mountains, where the wind and trees help me to hear my own intuition or my inner voice. The voice that I listened to when I was a child, before anyone taught me that I was separate from the "*big voice*" the "*God voice.*" You know that voice that rings in your ears when you are on the brink of jumping into something big and it yells, "*Yes! Yes! Go for it! You can do anything!*"

I have heard *the big voice* laughing a big belly laugh after I jumped and saying, "*I told you! you can do anything!*"

Near the end of my coaching career in 2008, I found myself sitting on an old dried-up tree stump, high in the mountains, overlooking the incredible Chinook Valley. I was watching the weather come rolling in over the mountain and then down and out through the valley floor. A couple of ravens were calling to each other and playing a game of 'who can be the most annoying.' Suddenly the wind behind me darkened, and it started to snow. Not a blizzard, just a huge dump of big fat snowflakes! The kind that when you were a kid you put your tongue out to catch. Watching the snowflakes helped me in pondering what to do. I had written all this information about coaching technique and about my view of how to enable people positively, but I just didn't know how to deliver my message. How would I tell everyone about my experience and what I had learned? That was when I heard the *big voice*, "*Helen? Seriously? Everyone has a story…just tell your story…just tell your story.*"

When I was little, the *big voice*, that *God voice* had a Santa Claus type of sound. I could swear this time the *big voice* had a slight hint of exasperation. The way your dad sounded when he tried to convince you that you were ready to take your driver's test. So, I listened to the *big voice* and I decided that in amongst all the coaching experiences and all the data I collected there was a story, my story.

So, I am going to tell you the story of my life of learning and leadership and all the travels through the peaks and valleys of that journey. Throughout that time, I collected data and created a coaching philosophy that I believe is worth repeating. I want to clarify that when I refer to "sport" in the general term I am using it in the context of participatory amateur sport.

I would like to separate out the business of sport and clarify that in that particular context the word "sport" is merely a description of an activity and its function is no different than being a stock broker or any other paid professional. The dynamics of that environment are based on business practices and do not reflect the general meaning of the word "sport" as it is intended in this book.

In conclusion, I would suggest that the guiding principle that I learned, and am suggesting in this book, could be applied in any coaching or leadership situation. The idea that we as humans are limitless and have simply adhered to belief systems that have not supported our dreams is not mine alone. There are many publications, and indeed, complete new age and self-help sections in the book stores, that reiterate this type of thinking. The story, however, is mine and I am happy to share it with the reader and hope that it is a meaningful and enjoyable read, and leads to a bit of 'barefoot flying…'

Helen Wright

Rugby Terms

The game of rugby is played by all people. All genders, all ages, throughout the world. Here are a few terms to help understand some of the plays.

15's game—the original game of rugby is played with 15 players for 80 minutes. The object of this group is to touch the ball down across the oppositions' goal line (try line in traditional rugby terms). You can do three things with the ball to move it down the field. You can kick it. You can carry it. You can pass it to another player who is lateral to yourself, so that they can carry it. You cannot pass the ball forward with your hands or your feet to another player who is in front of you.

Forwards—the team is made up of a group of eight forwards and seven backs. Forwards are the sturdy individuals whose skill set involves more pushing, lifting and wrestling. The positions are numbered one to eight. Props (numbered 1 and 3) are the two anchors on either side of a hooker (numbered 2). Those three comprise the front row. The hooker position is called that because that individual hooks the ball back to their own players with their feet when a scrummage has been called by the referee. There are two players behind the front row called, the second row (numbered 4 and 5). Their job is to push the front row forward in a scrummage. There are three individuals placed on either side and at the back of that group of five. They are called the back row. One flanker on each side (numbered 6 and 7) and another position (numbered 8) at the back. This back row are the first players to break off the scrum and attack the opposition or support their own backs.

Backs—the group of seven backs generally require speed, agility, and handling skills. The formation starts with a scrum half (numbered 9) who is the connector, moving the ball from the forwards (who contest for possession) to the rest of the backs, who are trying to score. The Standoff (numbered 10) is the quarterback of the attack or defense. There are two centers (numbered 12 and 13). They are the penetrators in attack and the tacklers in defense. There are two wingers and a fullback (numbered 11, 14 and 15). These three players are the final line of defense or the finishing speed in attack.

Scrummage—if you pass the ball forward or make any other technical errors, the game is stopped, and the opposition is given the opportunity to win possession of the ball through a contest called a "scrummage." A scrummage is similar to a hockey "face-off," except the ball is rolled in the middle of a controlled huddle and each hooker has the opportunity to hook the ball back to their own team. This formation is considered a "restart."

Lineout—if the ball rolls out of bounds, both teams again have the opportunity to contest for possession. This formation resembles a "jump ball" in basketball, except that in rugby the ball is thrown down the middle of a lineup of players. Two players are lifted into the air to try and transfer the ball back to their own team. This formation is also considered a "restart."

Penalties—for all infringements, personal or technical. The referee can award a penalty to the non-offending team. They have the opportunity to kick for points or field position or carry the ball forward unobstructed for ten meters.

7's game—the 7's game is a reduced version of the 15's game. It is played by seven players for 15 minutes. It is generally a fast-paced game conducive to tournaments and television. Currently there is a World Cup for both the 15's game and the 7's game.

Lexicon

A try—scoring points by crossing the end zone line and touching the ball down generates five points.

Back line—the formation of the players who are lined up in the back field to either receive the ball in attack mode or tackle the opposing players when they receive the ball.

Club level—rugby is played at several levels. Club level is community level open to everyone, regional level would be the selected representative team for a region, provincial level is representing a province and national level is selected to play for the national team.

First division—generally most leagues have one to three or four categories of competition. The first division would generally be the highest level of playing category.

Front row—the group name of the two props and hooker.

Hooker—position of the player located in the middle of the front row of the scrummage, who "hooks" the ball back to their own team.

Kava—Pacific Island drink that gets you high.

Lineout—A formation in the game of rugby that is used as a restart when the ball goes out of bounds.

Natural inside step—The intuitive ability of a player to step laterally in the opposite direction of where they were running.

Prop—position of the two players located on either side of the hooker in the scrummage, who hold the hooker in place and push against the opposition.

Scrummage—a formation in the game of rugby that is used as a restart when a technical infraction has occurred, and the referee has stopped the game.

Try line—the goal line across the ends of the field.

Number 8—position of the player located at the back of the scrummage who provides push to scrummage.

Chapter 1
In the Beginning
(September 1955–September 1970)

My story begins on September 19, 1955. I was born in the interior of British Columbia in a small town called Williams Lake. My parents, Martha and Adolph Beyerle, were German. My mother's name was Martha Weinert and my father's name was Adolph Beyerle. They weren't actually born and raised in Germany. They were Germans who were born around the Black Sea. My mom in Romania and my dad in the Ukraine. After World War I, Germans were offered land in exchange for developing agriculture in these areas. Many German families moved to these areas and developed successful farming operations. At the outset of World War II, Hitler called all these Germans to come back to Germany and work for the Third Reich. Most of the men went into the army and most of the women had to work in the factories. They survived the war but sought to relocate as quickly thereafter as circumstances would allow.

My dad had finally convinced my mother that Canada was the land of milk and honey. It was post-war Germany and both had survived the experience but not without an emotional price. In today's understanding of the consequences of war trauma, we would have labelled them as suffering from post-traumatic stress disorder. Because my mom had lost her first husband on the Russian front and her second child had been killed in her arms through sniper fire, she was more afflicted by the impact of the war than my dad.

Driven by the desire to find opportunities to own land, my dad originally applied to immigrate to various locations in South America. My mom was opposed to living in warm climates and continued to follow him to the immigration office and cancel all his applications, without his knowledge. The immigration people finally advised my father of the situation and he approached her to determine a location that would be acceptable to both.

Both of my parents came from large families. My mom's family consisted of five sisters and six brothers. My dad's family included six sisters and one brother. My dad's family had not been as fortunate as him in escaping to the west following the war and were banished to Siberia. This was a German family who had moved to Odessa after the First World War to develop the agriculture in that area. My dad's family did not respond to the call for all Germans to return to Germany in the same way that my mom's family did. My dad was the only living male in the family and he returned and joined the German army, but his sisters did not. Consequently, at the end of the war, it became apparent how Germans would fare under Stalin and my aunts and their families tried to leave Russia. They were not only turned back at the border but identified as Germans and sent to Siberia.

This is another story but suffice it to say that my dad's perception of Canada was always much more positive and hopeful. For him, it was a slice of heaven, while for my mother it was simply one ordeal after another.

In 1954, Mom and Dad landed by boat in Halifax and travelled across Canada on a train. They arrived in Halifax by boat and then took the train to St. Paul, Alberta, where they had agreed to be farm hands for the period of a year. That agreement covered the cost of their fare. They arrived in St. Paul in the winter of 1954. Even though she said that she was pregnant with me coming over to Canada, if you do the math, that can't be possible. They left St. Paul as soon as they could, which would have been the winter of 1955 and I was born in September 1955 in Williams Lake. She must have gotten pregnant at Christmas of 1954, just before my dad left to find work in B.C. My parents got off the train in St. Paul, Alberta, and my mom, wearing her best travelling dress, went directly to the barn to help with the milking.

They were in Alberta for the minimum of one year, which was part of the agreement I have referred to previously. My oldest sister remembers them leaving St. Paul in the winter, because she and my other sister had to stay until school was finished. My brother (five at the time) remembers staying in a skid shack out in the bush in the winter and finally catching a ride with a logging truck to Williams Lake.

After months of research into possible opportunities for work, my dad found his version of heaven in the interior of British Columbia. The land of loggers and ranchers helped to fulfill his dream of becoming John Wayne. He and his nephew John Weinert, who was my mom's nephew, found the perfect work for a hard-working German, loading lumber into box cars and paid by the linear foot. Work equals pay.

Following the dismantling of the Berlin Wall, we would reconnect with my dad's sisters and determine that their experience in Siberia and ours in the interior of British Columbia were almost identical with the exception that we had access to more wood. My dad often questioned my mother on her choice to bring goose down feather blankets with her from Germany, but she declared many times that those feather blankets saved the lives of her children more than once.

From this initiation to the B.C. frontier, my family carved out a dairy farm. That was where I spent my youth. This land of loggers and ranchers was the canvas for all the blueprints that would form my young psyche: Work equals pay; work equals love; there is no option, work must be done; there is always a way, sometimes it is just a bit harder; Quitting is not an option; work is genderless until it is time to be paid; hard laborious work can be eased by using your brain. My dad was an equal opportunity employer. He had to be because he had five girls and one boy. His wife and his children were by far the best workers he 'never' had to pay—ever! Needless to say, I grew up believing that I could do anything and from my parents' perspective, that was absolutely true.

My early years were spent in a Tom Sawyer/Huck Finn existence. My older sisters were eleven and thirteen years older than I was and my brother was five years older. That difference in age gave me the freedom to roam the fields and bushes of our farm completely unobstructed and immersed in a limitless imagination. I would follow the cows through the tunnels they carved through the thick underbrush and emerge into open meadows where the timothy grass grew wild and was high enough to provide me with complete camouflage. I wore little shabby running shoes, shorts, and T-shirts and the sensation of power in my legs and wind in my face, as I ran through the tall grass, propelled me to run everywhere. At five years old, I had no concept of fear and totally enjoyed this unending, sensory delight!

Our farm was nestled below the west hills of the Williams Lake valley. We called them mountains because that was how they felt when we were driving the cows out to pasture. Although my dad was a John Wayne "wannabe," we never obtained the services of a horse until my brother was old enough to convince my dad he could ride. In the meantime, short little stout running goats like myself provided invaluable services, skirting around the herd and chasing them up the mountain through the towering trees to higher pasture. We lived two miles from town, down a curvy little dirt road that wound its way over cattle guarded creeks and through two big hills. In the wintertime, it looked like a Christmas card with all the fire and spruce boughs covered in sparkling, soft, white snow.

Mr. Wotzky lived on the same road and was a blacksmith; complete with a fire oven, re-forming horse shoes and generally working magic with metal and his huge weathered brown hands. Mr. Wotzky had been a working cowboy and when he and his four sons came and helped us with branding and castrating, it was always as a favor to my dad. One winter, he built a horse-drawn sleigh, and before he delivered it to the purchaser, he came by our house and offered to take us for a ride. I can recall so vividly being tucked between him and his wife, under a blanket and feeling the crisp night wind on my face. The moon, the stars, the snow, the tinkle of the bells on the horses' harness and this incredible sense of belonging to this world.

In the summer, you could see my mom's green garden from the top of the first hill and at one point, we actually got the barn painted and I remember feeling a sense of pride at how lovely it looked. We lived in the same town that was home to the Williams Lake Stampede, which occurred every year on the first weekend in July. We were never allowed to attend the Stampede because that weekend was always the first cut of hay and it was imperative to get it cut, bailed, and stacked before the impending summer rain. I did actually attend one year when I was about five or six years old. My sister Inga and my brother Helmut were given permission to take me to the parade on the Saturday morning. My long-suffering siblings could only attend social functions (dates, parties, etc.) if they had me in tow. As I reflect, at the time that probably wasn't a bad strategy to deter most normal but questionable teenage behavior. We were at the Stampede Parade and I was so engaged with the pageantry and the local musical bands and the general excitement of the whole event that I was relentless in my pursuit of these pied pipers to the Stampede grounds and midway. Both Inga and Helmut knew this was outside the scope of what had been permitted, but surely an hour wouldn't be so bad? Remember that I told you that I was short? Remember that I told you I was fearless? Remember that I told you I had an unquenchable imagination? It was about lunch time when I noticed that my siblings were no longer within spotters' distance. I had been so engrossed in the world view from below three feet that I had completely forgotten about them. The world below three feet lets you watch the bull riding and bucking competition through the two bottom planks of the rider's chutes, being sprayed with dirt from the plunging hooves. The world below three feet lets you slip under the horses' bellies to scoot over to the midway rides and the intoxicating smell of burning sugar in the cotton candy machine. The world under three feet lets you climb the stairs to the announcer's booth and request that they call your sister Inga and your brother Helmut, who are lost, to come to the announcer's booth. The world under three feet does not have any concept of time, but it does have a concept of hunger. After what seemed an endless period of time, I decided that it was probably time I took things into my own hands and headed home. I knew the way. I had paid attention all the time that I had ridden in my dad's milk trucks. I wandered home, arriving in the late afternoon and demanded to know where Inga and Helmut were. I only remember one spanking in my life and now that I am a parent, I can only imagine the conflicting emotions of relief and anger that must have overcome my dad when he turned to see this three-foot-high blonde little goat with her hands on hips demanding an explanation.

As I grew taller, I graduated from the freedom of "wild child" to a contributing member of the family business. I was officially designated as "watcher of the cows." The position came with life-changing responsibilities and a horse. Molly was an old, fat, white mare that dad had traded with the guys at the Sugarcane Reserve (Williams Lake Band Reservation) for a truck load of hay. When he told them that he needed a 'safe' horse for his nine-year-old daughter to watch cows, the boys laughed out loud. "She will be OK with Molly," they said. "Molly has 'Indian' sense."

Apparently, when a horse has 'Indian sense,' they become so intuitive that they can sense when you want to catch them to ride and, just at the optimum moment, they race away. I spent the next six years of my life in a love-hate relationship with this animal that became my best friend. First of all, let me tell you that my dad's fears of me recklessly racing across the field at warp speed were completely alleviated when he saw Molly run. Moving Molly from a slow trot to a gallop required prodding bordering on abuse. It would not have been such an exercise in frustration if I didn't witness her capacity for blinding speed as she raced away from me having consumed the oats in the bucket and once again evading capture.

There were two things that happened in my life at this point. My older sisters exposed me to one of my greatest addictions…books, and my dad discovered that if you had a "watcher of cows," you didn't need fences. And so, every summer I spent my days herding cows to various sites where they could feast throughout the day. During this period of feasting, I would sprawl on Molly's broad back and enter the worlds of Huckleberry Finn, Heidi and Little Women. I would become so engrossed in the stories that I wouldn't notice the cows moving into the "*No Go*" zones of alfalfa and oat hay fields. I would look up to see the swishing tails of black and white cows happily munching on what was supposed to be their winter feed!

"*Oh No!* Come on Molly! Run dam it run!"

She would look at me with those horse eyes clearly saying, "Make me!"

"Oh God! *Oh* God! I am going to be in so much trouble! Not paying attention *again!*"

This is where nature provided me with the greatest motivation to create aerobic capacity...*fear*. I would hop off Molly's back and sprint across the meadow and frantically herd the cows back into their approved eating area. Returning to where I had left Molly, she would lift her head and give herself a little stretch and decide that she was done with this nonsense and start trotting off home. The number of times that Molly arrived in the yard followed by me on foot with a herd of very full and happy cows became the source of great glee in my family. I would arrive in the farm house, hot, tired, sticky from the heat and furious. My mom and dad could hardly contain their gurgling laughter as they would ask me unnecessary questions about the course of events from my afternoon. Clearly, the horse was smarter than me, *what do you need to know? I am in training!*

Well, if Molly was responsible for my aerobic capacity, my job as "pail carrier" was providing all the core and upper body strength I would require for a lifetime of rugby. In those days, milking cows was not the elaborate electronic process that it is today. Cows were driven into stalls, their tails were tied up with hanging strings of binder twine, their teats were washed with a bucket of water and soap and sucking machines were applied. Once it was apparent that their milk bags were empty, the machines were emptied into stainless steel buckets and carried from the barn to the dairy house and emptied into strainers and then lifted and poured over the cooler. My progression into the working world of the family business started with herding and then moved along to 'tail tier,' 'teat washer,' and 'shit shoveler.' Even though we had a 'barn cleaning' machine, it never worked. The only thing that worked with consistency was one person shoveling shit into the wheelbarrow and one person pushing the wheelbarrow out of the barn and emptying it. It was a job reserved for the two with the least amount of seniority, myself and my brother. I don't remember fondly, but I do remember that my brother took particular delight in finding the most fluid cow shit he could find and launching it into the wheelbarrow so that it would splash on me. There were a few moments of retribution when the roles would reverse, but again it would involve a sprint to the protecting circumference of my mother's working space.

The moment that I grew tall enough to have one-inch clearance under the pail, I was elevated to the lofty position of "pail carrier." This meant that I carried not only five-gallon pails of milk to the dairy house, it meant that I also carried five-gallon pails of ground grain to feed the cows. This work occurred 365 days of the year in the 30-plus-degree-heat of summer to the -30 degree-cold of winter. I wasn't the only one in my family who did this work, I was just the shortest. Maneuvering over steps and bumps meant shrugging my shoulders to gain the height I needed for clearance. Lifting the milk cans to pour over the cooler meant that I had to get the can up on my knee and then use my knee to hoist the can over my head without spilling the milk. The wonderful thing about work is that there really isn't any choice. It has to be done and so it is. Sometimes what you do becomes who you are.

Part of who I am is the result of the influence of one person in my formative years in elementary school. Hazel Huckvale was a stout, stocky, redheaded, Scottish woman, who happened to be my principal for the first seven years of my education. Hazel was the principal of Glendale Elementary School. Glendale Elementary School was located not only on the wrong side of town but on the wrong side of the tracks, right beside the mill and closer to the garbage dump than the town. Needless to say, the attendees of Glendale elementary were not the children of the town's professional core. No, they were native kids, whose parents floated in and out of their shanty homes and they were East Indian kids whose parents didn't speak English. The white kids who attended that school had questionable lineage and never experienced dwellings without wheels. How Hazel ever convinced Martha Beyerle that her little blonde bundle of attitude would receive a better education from her than anywhere else is proof of her passion. Hazel's mission in life was to ensure that Glendale Elementary School and anyone who attended therein, would be provided with the best education that she could deliver. And deliver she did! Hazel never wore pants and Hazel's shoes always had strong stocky heals that echoed through the halls of the school providing a clear warning of her presence. If micromanage was a word back then, she would have been the resident expert. She ruled over her hen house with a loud brogue accent that carried throughout the halls providing information for anyone who might not be absolutely clear who was in charge. She accepted no excuses and she tolerated nothing but anyone's very best. It wasn't that she wasn't empathetic for the situations of the many students that found their way to her desk; she understood completely, the plethora of life's limitations. She simply didn't accept them as an impediment to her goal, which was our growth and development. She loved music and so we sang! She loved drama and so we wrote our own plays and performed! Glendale Elementary School was renowned in the school district for winning almost all of the categories of the Kiwanis choir and oral speaking competition. We only ever lost to the Sugarcane Mission School in oral speaking because they really had the lock on monotone and meter. We secretly agreed that even Hazel might have shared our fear of those nuns! Hazel was not a real sports fan, but when the other schools organized floor hockey, we were in and she was there! She organized our transportation to tournaments and participation was not an option. You breathed, you played. Parents were in mortal fear of having Hazel come to their house to find her students. More than once, we witnessed the meanest, baddest, hard drinking logger pull up to the school in his rig and drop off his equally bad assed kid, just to ensure he didn't have to face the wrath of Hazel. In terms of educational performance, she gave no quarter and she provided no escape route that didn't involve a sound understanding of the material. It was the very first time that I experienced the expectation of achievement that was supported by her time, her will, and her undying belief in us. All of us. She convinced all of us that her belief should be our belief and that became the cornerstone for all things possible.

As I mentioned, my parents were immigrants. Though they had mastered the English language in terms of speaking, they were challenged in the reading and writing department. So, when Hazel convinced them that I was bright with a limitless future, they accepted my abilities to translate with great confidence.

But first let me catch you up on the history of events that occurred throughout that period of time. My parents had invested all that German work, energy, and enthusiasm into building a thriving dairy business. My dad was the skillful salesman and a visionary. We sold and delivered chocolate milk before most stores could get it from the big creameries. As soon as milk cartons became vogue, my dad had a machine and we were on the cutting edge providing pasteurized, homogenized, and skim milk. We had cream and chocolate milk, we had trucks and drivers, and we had tokens. What we didn't have was control of those tokens. Because of their inability to read and track their cash flow they became the sad example of what victims of a drunk, cheating accountant lookalike. They lost it all. That could have been the end but that simply is not in the fiber of Martha and Adolph Beyerle. There is no "going bankrupt" and there is no "giving up." And so, they made a deal with the bank to repay all of the outstanding balance and we became "ranchers." We moved from black and white Holstein cows to red and white Herefords.

As though life hadn't already dealt my parents enough bad hands, in the September of 1967, my sister Inga was killed in a car crash on her way to teachers' college in Seward, Nebraska. They never really recovered from that. My brother, at that time, was entering into the new world of drugs and seemed to be a constant source of grief and legal trouble. He believed that both of them wished it had been him and not Inga. In honesty, he was probably right. He found a motor bike and hit the road to experience his version of "Easy Rider." My oldest sister Erika, after all those debilitating years of lifting milk cans and operating the pasteurizing process, finally escaped Williams Lake to become a nurse, working in the Montreal Children's Hospital. So that left me, and my two younger sisters Lolita and Loni.

My two younger sisters were born in 1962 and 1964. Lolita was a precious little dark eyed, dark haired ball of energy. She was seven years younger than me and immediately became my responsibility, as I had been my older sisters' responsibility. My older sisters had picked her name from an exotic book and she would come to fulfil that passionate type of personality. My mom was forty-four years old when Elona (Loni) was born. She was born with Downs' Syndrome and became the one individual in our family that everyone loved unconditionally.

When a tragedy occurs in a family, the loosely threaded seams that previously held the bonds of a family unit together, tear apart. If my mom's perception that my dad was the source of her misery existed before, it now expanded to include the death of her daughter. If the relationship between my dad and my brother had been strained before, it was now in full blown confrontation. If I had an inclination to leave this place, it was now a solidified goal.

And so, we began again, a little more cynical and certainly more restricted from a monetary perspective. If we weren't poor farmers before, we were now in the category of 'dirt poor.' The wonderful thing about work is that it can take your mind off your problems and let you focus in on something that has the potential to be hopeful. And so, we worked. We built fences on that mountain through gullies and ditches that would be dangerous for most cattle to scramble through, much less our towing barbed wire through.

The beautiful little dairy farm that lay nestled in the belly of surrounding hills was actually owned by the PGE (Pacific Great Eastern Railway, later known as the BCR, British Columbia Rail). My dad rented the five hundred valley acres that provided our home and our hay from the railway. It was an annual lease. Over the years, just about the same time that he would clear the land and have it ready for planting, the railway guys from Vancouver would come and tell him that they were cutting yet another piece of property from his lease. They were building another mill. It didn't take very long for our closest neighbors to be a 24-hour screeching, smoke belching, air polluting mega-plywood plant. So, when my church-going parents started stealing small generators and pumps from the mill's vast inventory to move water onto their now reduced hay fields, I simply concluded that they, those rich people, deserved it because they were evil. It is somewhat ironic that through many of the interactions that I had with corporate, wealthy people from that point on, I seldom encountered evidence to challenge that belief.

After we lost the dairy business and my sister was killed, my mom avoided anything that remotely resembled risk. She took control of her own world and held on to some milking cows and chickens and proceeded to sell milk and eggs from the farm. It was illegal to sell 'raw' products in the market, so all of her customers came to her. She collected what she called 'peklas.' A 'pekla' was a small pile of five- and ten-dollar bills wrapped in a twenty-dollar bill equal to hundred dollars. She would hide her 'peklas' in various locations through the house but mostly under her mattress. At that point, my dad and I became business partners. I was accepted as the official translator and voice of 'his' or rather 'our' ventures. Because the business was now about ranching and not milking, the cows had to be driven from our yard in the spring to the higher pastures. But because cows are not stupid, they would continually find their way down to the emerald, succulent alfalfa fields at the bottom of the mountain. It was an ongoing dance. We would chase them up. They would come down. We would chase them up. Mom would follow behind us in the truck and agree to meet us at a particular point to give us a ride back down. She would wait for five minutes…we would be longer…she would leave. We would have to walk back down the mountain. It was on these afternoon walks back down the mountain that we created the dreams that fueled my father's imagination and my entrepreneurship. Our favorite game was "How would you spend a million dollars?" The first rule to being an entrepreneur is that you have to have dreams. The second rule to being an entrepreneur is that you have to learn how to play the "game."

The "game" usually involves two types of strategies; the first strategy applies to all things government—*never, never* tell them more than what they are asking for! *Always,*

always show that you are contributing! *Never, never* show that the venture might be very successful, only ever marginal. *Always, always* make sure that they believe they are smarter than you and that they are doing you a favor!

The very first time that my dad sent me to the B.C. Land Office in pursuit of an agricultural lease, he said to me, "Hella, you go in *der und* you play dumb. You tell *dem dat you* dad sent you to get *da* papers and *dat* you don't know *vat* papers and how you gonna fill *dem* out."

I looked at him incredulously and answered, "Dad, that is not me playing dumb. It's the actual truth. I *don't* know!"

"Yah, yah," he answered. "Now go."

So off I went, and it played out exactly as he had mapped it out. They were extremely helpful and delighted to show me all of the nuances to successfully completing the application. That relationship between myself and the Lands Office guy provided us with the title to three-quarter sections of saleable timber. I was sixteen years old.

The second strategy involves the financial community; generally, a group of individuals who lack authority to affect change but enjoy the idea of power—this group of individuals are more fearful and less helpful than the government folks. Make sure your paperwork is solid! *Always* make sure they have something for collateral! It doesn't have to be real but it has to look real and you have to be ready to explain it all! Make sure that the risk you are taking looks like no risk at all! *Always, always* show them your Plan B! It appears to me that creative accounting people are in business, not banks. *Always, always* have a real Plan B! Whatever you do. Always provide them with the knowledge that they have the power and are doing you a favor! *Never, never* challenge their authority!

A sixteen-year-old cannot go to the bank. It just isn't credible in their traditional world. But a sixteen-year-old can learn how to create a business plan and a budget. We needed to buy cows. It was the corner stone to our revenue plan. So, my dad and I sat down and logically mapped out how this cow buying venture was actually going to work and then we converted that information into a financial document. It was rudimentary, but it only contained totals. The formulas behind the totals were a well-rehearsed performance that my dad had down to a fine art. I made an appointment for him and he was scheduled to attend the office of the Royal Bank in Williams Lake. Before he left, he looked at his reflection in the mirror, tilting his grey Stetson. "Today, Hella, I gonna kiss *dat* banker's ass, and *dats* OK because next week, we gonna go to *de* auction."

He came away with a line of credit for ten thousand dollars using every single asset he owned and a personal guarantee. He then borrowed five thousand dollars more from his life insurance policy and he was absolutely correct. The next week, we went to the auction.

Before I advance any further, I want to tell you about the three people in my life who have supported me unconditionally, regardless of what the current passion might have been. My oldest sister Erika operated in the capacity of a mother, even before my own mother could no longer cope with that reality. After the age of five (baby cuddling age), my mother could no longer engage in physical contact with her children. She wanted to, but something in experience simply denied her that freedom.

My oldest sister, who was technically old enough to be our mother, stepped in and provided the care and attention that we all required. She was the checker of marks, the questioner of decisions, the compass for sailing into the world of friends and who was worth keeping and who should be discarded. She drove us crazy! Even when we had our own children, every time we met, there was report card time and an accounting of our physical, financial, and emotional well-being. Most importantly, she made up for every hug that we didn't get from my mother.

When Lolita was born, I was seven years old and I thought she was the most beautiful baby I had ever seen. She had my dad's dark complexion, a full head of dark, curly hair and big round brown eyes. My older sisters must have thought the same thing because they named her Lolita. And she delivered all the attitude and presence that name infers. She was exotic. Five years after Lolita was born, my sister Inga died and my mom simply exchanged one brown eyed beauty for another. My mother took my older sister's clothes and sewed them into reduced sizes that would fit Lolita. She insisted that Lolita take piano lessons and learn to sing, replicating the talents of my sister Inga. She would often call Lolita by Inga's name and cut her hair to resemble Inga. Lolita spent most of her formative young life fighting for her own persona and trying to distance herself from a sister she didn't even remember. Like all dreams, Lolita hung unto hers and finally manifested what the Dixie Chicks had promised her: *Cowboy Take Me Away*. Lolita was the grounding rod that prevented me from destroying myself in self-judgment.

And then there was Elona, or Loni, as we called her. She was the one thread that held the entire dysfunctional group together. Loni was born in 1964 when my mom was forty-four years old. She was born with down syndrome and croup (a breathing disorder). At her birth, some backwoods doctor suggested that it might be in her best interest to simply let her pass away. My mom had to physically restrain my dad from tearing the imprudent professional from limb to limb. Her life expectancy at the beginning was no more than a year. Then it was certainly no more than ten. Absolutely not past 16. Certainly not further than 20. Elona Beyerle has outlived both her parents, a sister, and a brother and continues to show up every day with the same inspiring smile and zest for life with which she was born. She is a living example of goodness, unless, of course, she doesn't get her coffee at three, then she can be a living example of pissed right off. She loves us all unconditionally because she doesn't know how to love any other way, and I strive daily to pay that forward.

So, how did I get from a dairy farm in Williams Lake to coaching rugby? It is an interesting road map. I remember telling my mother about this game that I had become involved with.

"Hella, *vat* kinda shit you are talking about? You are playing *mit rutabagas*? *Vat* kinda people play *mit rutabagas*?"

"No, Mom. it is called rugby. It is a game."

"Na, who plays *dis* game?"

"Men. Men and boys."

"Ya *und* do girls play?"

"Well, they didn't before, but they do now."

"Varum? *Vy*? You don't have anything else you can do?"

"Mom, I kind of like it."

"So *vy* do you like it?"

"Well, I get to tackle people."

"*Vat* is tackle?"

"Hit, you know, like in wrestling. Put people on the ground."

"*Ach du lieber!* Hella, you are crazy! You *vant* to hit something, I gonna give you some *vork* and *den* we gonna see if you *vant* to hit anything!"

In trying to explain this situation to my dad, my mom's picture of me running around a field randomly hitting people with rutabagas got the best of her and she disintegrated into fits of giggles. Between the two of them, a healthy glass of Kelowna Red, and pictures of me chasing vegetables around a field, they buckled into full out, uncontainable belly laughs. That was another component of my childhood, humor!

I was never allowed to participate in any organized sport when I was in Williams Lake. We lived on a farm, so staying late for any kind of practice meant someone would have to drive to town and pick me up; not happening. The main reason that any kind of participation in sport was not happening was because it did not involve work. In fact, it got in the way of work and work was the primary motivation to life. It might sound like I was somehow deprived, but I didn't really feel that way. There was nothing about sport from my experience in phys-ed classes that would have made me think I was missing some wonderful experience. The process for picking teams was a constant reminder to me that not only was I a bonafide nerd, but a complete outcast in the realm of sport. Always the last and reluctant pick, I soon learned that sport was only for the chosen few, those endowed with visible capacity (speed, height) or those endowed with skill sets that most of us had not been privy to.

My dream in those early years was to follow in the footsteps of my two favorite characters, Tammy (from the Gidget movies, played by Sandra Dee) and Maria (from the Sound of Music, played by Julie Andrews). If I could be like those characters, I too could find my way to romance, freedom and happiness. It didn't take me too long to figure out that I needed to move from this male-dominated environment typical to cowboys and loggers to one that allowed me more latitude. Being smart can trump work. Education and the advantages it can provide were not lost on my parents, and so I managed to obtain my parents approval to follow my older sister Inga's route to Concordia College in Edmonton, Alberta.

It was a well-supported idea, the thought of me going to Concordia College. But after having supported my sister Inga to go, there simply wasn't any money in the coffers for even the bus ride. If I was going to make my way in the wide, wide world, I was going to have to find the funds to do it. Inga had, previous to her death, provided me with all the information that I would require to survive in that new urban and academic environment. I just had to get there! I was on a mission. I wrote letters about scholarships. I wrote letters about bursaries. Through all of this communication, I finally arrived at the unpublished piece of crucial information that allowed a tiny ray of miracle light to shine through. Concordia College was a Lutheran school. A Lutheran school, dedicated to the creation of ministers, teachers and deacons and deaconesses. What is a deaconess? Whatever it is, I could be one of those! I originally wanted to be a minister, but through the many years of tortuous confirmation classes, Pastor Ruf had finally convinced me to accept that the Lutheran Church (Missouri Synod) did not allow women to be ministers, regardless of the fact that I was by far the best speaker on our confirmation day. But I could play this 'deaconess' card! And so, I did. With the same spirit that we bought those cows, I decided to jump first and figure out the details later! On September 1 1970, I boarded a Greyhound bus headed for Edmonton, Alberta. The Lutheran Church (Missouri Synod) paid for all my instruction through Grade 10 to my second year of university. I cleaned bathrooms, babysat professors' kids, worked in the library and any other job I could get my hands on to pay for my accommodation and spending money. The closest I got to being a deaconess was winning the election for spiritual coordinator on the students' council. That year the daily "Chapel Sermonettes," for which I was responsible, had the highest attendance ever! We rocked! They really should have just let me be a minister!

It was at Concordia that sport played an integral part of my life and carried me through my teenage years. Most of us at the school lived in residence and most of us were from religious Lutheran farming communities throughout B.C., Alberta, and Saskatchewan. We had little money, lots of free time and access to a gym. We played basketball. There were only 200 students in the entire high school program, so making the basketball team required the desire to do so and the time to acquire a few skills. I had plenty of both. It was the first time that I experienced the connectedness and comradery that can accompany team sport.

There were some lessons that later influenced my philosophies of coaching. Because of my unlimited access to the gym and basketballs and because I had nowhere else to be and nothing to do, I was the queen of the three-point shot. I could shoot baskets from anywhere on the court. I should have been a star! The only problem was that I could only shoot those baskets when there was no one in front of me. I practiced alone, without any opposition, and so I could only be sensational alone; without any opposition. I adapted quickly and became relatively proficient but never as good as I was in a game of 'horse' or '21.' My limitations became apparent pretty quickly. Too short, too slow. Basketball is not supposed to be a contact sport and, in those days, girls didn't wrestle. It was, however, a very satisfactory experience and allowed me elevation from my nerd status and entry into the 'jock' world. I was very lucky to spend my teenage years in the comforting folds of a small Lutheran high school. I don't have any stories of abusive nuns or bullying roommates. We were all confused, horny teenagers, sneaking into dormitories and falling in and out of love on a regular basis. Our goals were to reach university and build those abundant lives that none of us had ever experienced firsthand. We were under the watchful eyes of elderly professors and compassionate dorm parents, and managed to survive our puberty without any great duress.

I moved from high school to university, to work, to marriage, to kids, and finally found myself exposed to this community of people who not only played rugby, but were dedicated to spreading the gospel of this most unusual activity. And so, it began, my most wonderful love affair with a game that is so much more than the overt activity of throwing a rutabaga around.

Chapter 2
From Player to Coach (1977–1988)

My first husband, Scotty, was a rugby player. He was a rugby player in every sense of the word. His whole world was consumed with the sport. When I first met him, he made it clear to me that if I were to engage in a competition between his sport and his love for me, I would lose. I have always been an independent soul, unafraid of my own company, so I found that less offensive than most. I was also mildly impressed with his commitment to this strange activity and somewhat intrigued by the game and the community.

I came to enjoy the dynamics and personality of this community. It was composed of young boys to old men. There didn't appear to be any particular socio-economic strata that dominated the cross section of members. They ranged from students to fire fighters, laborers, lawyers and professors. Nor did there seem to be a 'body type.' They were big and robust, tall and lanky, small and stout, small and lean, and everything in between. What an odd collection of humanity. They all seemed to be extremely passionate about their participation in this endeavor. There was also an uncanny respect for every level of participant. The very elite players were no more valued than the beginners, and all were susceptible to the testosterone-laden repartee that passed for humor. If I didn't know better, I would have thought they actually cared very much for each other.

There has been a tradition throughout the world of rugby that encourages teams to travel throughout the world, playing and being hosted by other teams. This tradition provides an opportunity for the hosting team to billet players in their homes. It eliminates the cost of accommodation and food and creates an opportunity for friendship and reciprocal visits.

And so, it went. Scotty and I hosted young players from Britain's snobbiest private schools to sheep farmers from New Zealand and they all slept in our unfinished basement. They all drank copious amounts of beer. They all ate incredible amounts of food and they all expressed the same authentic appreciation for anything that we could provide for them on their journey. But most of all, they shared that undeniable love for this game that they all played and it allowed them to communicate at a level that transcended any barriers.

I was quite happy to support this lifestyle. I was never bored. I was always respected for who I was and most importantly there was a plethora of 'boy candy' to keep my eyes occupied. When I did start to get bored with watching my husband play, I would beg off by stating that I never was a very good spectator and that without the opportunity to play it had little interest for me. At that point, I was quite convinced that females did not participate in this game and so would be quite safe with my rather ingenious escape route.

On a very inconsequential day, I was repeating my reason for escaping into my own world when Scotty looked at me with an expression of sheer delight. With the same enthusiasm as a lottery winner, he sputtered that there was indeed a women's team that had been formed and now I too could participate in the most wonderful experience known to man! Needless to say, I was shocked and stunned. Trying to recreate the same level of enthusiasm, I uttered, "Great!" "Wow. Yeah, great!"

Clearly, there needed to be a rethinking of my game evasion strategy, so it occurred to me that the next escape route would have to involve an injury. Good plan! I would participate until I sustained an injury and then I would have a noble exit. Ironically, at the time I had no idea that this small piece of strategic insight would later give me some of the best coaching insight in terms of player psyche, relative to fear of failure. We can innocently create the opportunity for failure by simply thinking about an event long enough. If I am injured, I will not have to face that maybe I am not fit enough or face the fear that maybe I am frightened of the contact or not good enough to be part of a team. An injury can be a legitimate alternative to facing our fears. If I thought about it long enough, I could create the legitimate justification for the exit route.

I began to train with the only women's team in the city, the Edmonton Rockers. They were and still remain the only self-sustaining women's club in Alberta and possibly Canada. Suitable to their name, these girls rocked! Nothing that the Rockers have ever done has been without that unsinkable enthusiasm and self-belief that propelled all women's rugby forward at a time when that idea seemed impossible. The women that initiated rugby in Alberta were entirely independent. They raised their own money. They bought their own shirts. They created their own competition in Calgary. They organized their own games. They found their own coaches. They built their own clubhouse. They created their own vision for regional and provincial teams. They got themselves onto boards and created their own opportunities. In all that time between 1977 and 1988, I was never injured, nor did it occur to me to apply my exit strategy. At that point, I was completely and totally under the spell of this new life called "rugby."

Around 1982, one of my dear friends and also one of our coaches, Stan Dilworth, suggested that given the number of girls that were signing up, we should form another club. Hands flew into the air with emphatic gestures of resistance! But Stan and Corrine, Ruth and I, along with a few others went outside for a puff and carefully dissected the idea. It could double our playing time. We could be in charge of our own futures. We could do whatever we wanted! And so, it began.

We determined at the outset that we required the services of administratively competent females who could act in the capacity of president. Over the course of time many exceptional, professional women stepped up and guided our organization and development. Dave Graham helped us with the name and the logo. "You'll be bitches. uh. I mean witches," he laughed with his soft Glaswegian accent. "How about a collection of witches? How about the coven?" Sold!

And so, it began. Stephanie moved up from Calgary and anchored the back row at number 8. I directed traffic in the front row at Hook. Ruth terrorized the opposition at open field flanker. Terry was human cannon ball on the other side of the field. Corrine created the magic that was Scrum half, delivering the ball to our power center, Anne, who could kick the eyes out of sparrows and run through brick walls, with Bernadette and Judy on the wings. We attracted some outstanding athletes who were gay, and who appreciated the opportunity to play a physically challenging game, without the fear of judgment. It didn't hurt that both Ruth and Corrine's boyfriends were British guys doing their doctorates at the physical education department at the University of Alberta and offered to coach us. At the height of our success, barring the size factor, we had a back line that could easily contend with any of the local men's first division teams. Just so we are clear, a back line in rugby would be the same as a quarterback, with three running backs and a receiver all running in the same direction passing to each other laterally.

Once the girls in Calgary found out that a team was being formed in Edmonton, they proceeded to create their own team in Calgary, called the Renegades. So, with the Rockers and the Coven in Edmonton and the Renegades in Calgary, we started looking for opportunities to excel. There is safety in numbers and so part of the recruiting plan was to volunteer to coach girls' rugby in high schools. It was an easy sell. The wonderful thing about intelligent, driven women is that it didn't take them very long to infiltrate the existing bureaucracy and plant the seeds of championship.

We traded work for support. We will push your paper, do your bingos and organize your schedules if you support our request for a national championship! Done and done! We would like to be accepted as members of the local unions (organized leagues) Whaaaat? We will pay. Done and done! We would like to create an Alberta Provincial Women's Representative team? Whaaaaat!!! No, there is no money. By having women play rugby, you could double your government funding? We will do the paperwork. Done and done!

Whenever I am asked about what I think was the primary factor in convincing these staunch men's clubs to let women in and actually give them a vote, I think it is the simplest of explanations. First, just like my dad, no one can object to free labor. And then, of course, parties are way more fun when the girls can come! So all-around, they just liked having us there.

And so, it began. Soon the men's clubs were being asked by their own daughters about creating teams for girls. Saying no to a stranger is easy, saying no to your most cherished flesh and blood is not. And, if you are going to let them play, then let's make sure they have the opportunity to win! And soon, it is just no big deal. Everyone plays, just as it was divinely intended!

Playing at a local level with your friends and your fathers is not a difficult sell, but being allowed to play at an international level takes some real friends in high places. One of my best friends in life and in rugby is Barry Giffen. He is the epitome of 'good guy.' Not only does he support everyone to play rugby, but his nature is that he just generally supports everyone in most things. His heart is as big as the Canadian landscape and bleeds Maple Leaf red in any sport. He was an elite volleyball player at the University of Alberta and converted to rugby when he graduated. He is a natural leader because his ego has never found its way to the top of his priority list. Barry became the Canadian rugby union president the year the first Canadian women's team was selected and scheduled to play against the American women as a curtain raiser for the men's international test match in Victoria in the summer of 1987. The story is folk lore now, but it was his task to respond to the American captain's comment of women bastardizing the game of rugby. With the diplomatic ease of a senior statesman, Barry stood up and indicated that Canadians, in particular those Canadians that play rugby, support the game for everyone in Canada, including women and that everyone should get used to that fact and embrace the concept rather than denigrate this really great game! And with that said, we launched into the era of international rugby for women! Bravo Barry!

Throughout the period of time that I learned to play rugby, and played at the club, regional, and provincial level, I enjoyed every minute of it. There was always this sense of inclusion that had originally attracted me to the game. Sometimes we won, sometimes we lost, but most importantly we always played. Some people were faster, some were stronger, some were more skillful or smarter, and some people were leaders through sheer determination to stay on the field. Not everyone started, but everyone finished.

By contrast, my experience on that first national team was the worst sporting experience I have ever experienced. It took me twenty to thirty years to repair the damage from that encounter and some days I still get triggered back to those 'not good enough' moments. Selection, we were told was going to be determined through the performances shown throughout the games at the Canadian national women's championships (a competition between all the provincial representative teams to determine a national champion). The Alberta team not only won every game and the championship title, but did so with relative ease. The most challenging game was against Quebec, which had a formidable pack (similar in function to the front line of a football team). At this point, I was a mother of two children and tipping slightly past thirty years of age. I was, however, still the stout, strong, tough goat I had always been. Knowing that being smart trumps physical force, I had also pulled information specific to my position from every senior puffy eared veteran who had secrets to share and used them enhance my performance. I had won almost every contest for possession of the ball and I had carried that possession to provide the platforms for scoring that were expertly finished by our talented back line. When the hooker (position of the person in the middle of that front line who hooks the ball back to her team with her feet, similar in function to a hockey faceoff) from Quebec was named to the starting lineup, I was stunned. I was so confused. *How could that be? Hadn't I met all the criteria that had been outlined? Hadn't we won? Hadn't I clearly defeated my opposition? Isn't that what they said I had to do?* I am a female of German descent and I can assure you that self-criticism is a big strong molecule in that DNA helix, so the idea that I somehow missed my own subpar performance was simply not a possibility. At the same time that I was reeling from shock, there was great jubilation in the room. The announcement had been the capping moment of the entire weekend and meant to celebrate the great success of women's rugby. You have to remember that for me, this was the very first time that I had encountered this type of experience complete with the cacophony of opposing emotions. Girls were hugging me and expressing their great joy that we were all on the team and that we were finally going to play on the international stage. I didn't have a lot of experience in sport but I knew enough from my high school basketball that no one is terribly excited about being on the bench. And yet, somehow, I got this feeling that I should be so grateful! The coaches continued to express how pleased they were with my performance and how delighted they were to be taking all of us to Victoria. *If they were so pleased how come they didn't pick me?* They did pick me! Just not to start. *What the hell?* I would later find out that the actual reason for my bench allocation was that I was thirty plus and this new young hooker from Quebec could provide many more years of performance, paying greater dividends on their coaching investment. Ironically, I never saw her again after that year. So began the creation of my negative self-belief. When I reflect now, I think that the most damaging part of the entire experience is the expectation that you deny all your hurt and confused emotions and carry on pretending that you are grateful to be part of this great team and this great experience. This great experience, that really isn't so great for you. You drank the high performance "cool aid." You bought into the "if you work hard and beat your opposition, you will be chosen" lie. You worked so hard and did your part and now it is time for "them" to do theirs, which is to pick you! It's quite simply not fair! Welcome to high performance! Your first lesson is that "fair" is not an expectation for anyone in this realm.

As a bench player, you are not included in the unit preparation unless you are the token opposition, you are not included in the team run through, unless you are the token opposition and you are not privy to the coach's asides designed only for those chosen special ears. I sound like a jealous schoolgirl! I know! But that is because I am a female who was brought up in a society that pits us all against each other! I don't know how to feel anything else? I *am* jealous! That should be me! You told me the rules and I played by them and then you changed them and now I feel cheated and I am so 'effing mad! But even being mad is bad! I am supposed to somehow find some gratitude in not being picked and be a good girl and good team player and not tell anyone how really, really pissed I am. Ultimately, other than being a "real sore loser" and simply going home, the only way to digest this situation is to accept that they must be right and that you are simply not good enough, and your judgment is flawed. I so clearly remember feeling like that little nerd in those Williams Lake junior high school Phys Ed classes. The last, reluctant pick.

The game was played, we lost. I remember looking at the American prop who was sporting an Iroquois haircut and had the sleeve of her jersey rolled up tightly around her huge bicep. That was the only moment that I thought the bench might not be so bad after all. Growing up on my parent's farm did not allow for the option of quitting and so I decided that if I weren't good enough, I would simply have to buckle down and get good enough. The one area that the coaches reflected to me for improvement was my aerobic capacity and my speed. Running. I needed to be able to run further and faster.

Following this perplexing and devastating experience, I internalized the assessment that I was not good enough to play at this level or on this national team. At this point, I was now a mother of two children, in my mid-thirties. I went home for a summer to help my family and I was determined to rectify any short coming that might prevent me from being good enough. So, I started running. Everywhere. I created a running route that involved a logging road that ran along the circumference of our farm and required a significant climb at the base of the mountain. I would start out each morning from the back of the barn. My mom would look at me and laugh, "You *vant* I should come *mit* you?"

Funny, Mom, very funny. Off I would go, over the creek, up the road past the pond, hook up with logging road and up that enormous hill. It was a dirt road cut out of the side of a clay-based hill. Because of the incline, the trees were sparse and there was only prickly bush on the down side of the road. I am not sure if the word got out to every dam logger in the area that there was some blonde thing running on the road that made a good target and if nothing else a good laugh to start the day. I would approach the road and scan to see if any trucks were in the vicinity. Ear to the ground. No rumbling. Hit it, Helen! It never failed every time I was halfway up; some greasy-haired, manic looking bastard would switch gears and gun it, holding off to the last second to blast his air horn and run me off the road. I would tumble down into the prickle bushes feeling the heat of the truck engines blast by me. I started earlier; they came earlier. I started later; they came later. Finally, I figured out that the only way to win this war was to beat them to the top of the hill. Throughout the summer, I got closer and closer until finally near the end of the summer it happened. I started out feeling pretty damn fast. Shades of my early childhood came back when running was just something I did to feel the power of my legs and the wind in my face. I got to the road. It was a hot, sunny day and a little bit later so the sun had already moved halfway up the hill and baked the road into a fine dust. Rather than preserve my air supply I started running at a faster pace at the very bottom of the hill. I was about half way up when I thought that maybe there would be no "truck event" today, but suddenly I heard him changing gears. I was a little further along so he had to really push the gas pedal and the roar of his engine echoed through the whole valley. Cows lifted their heads to see what the commotion was about. Game on asshole! I started sprinting two thirds of the way up and I could hear him gaining. The roar continued to fill my ears and I could feel the rumbling of the ground as he bounced that rig over every rut on the road. I could start to smell the dust from his tires. All of sudden, every ounce of anger that I had ever pushed deep within me surfaced and my legs responded to the surge of adrenalin with sheer force. It's a moment that taught me that the brain tries to convince the body of all its limitations but the body under its own direction has a much greater capacity than most of us believe. I pounded my way to the top of the hill pumping my arms so hard that my fingernails dug deep into my clenched fists. I reached the top of the hill just in time to raise both hands in a double-fingered salute as he flew by me laughing out of an open window.

Some days when I lack motivation, I go back to that hill and listen for the rumble of that logging truck and the laughter through an open window.

I returned to the next national team selection camp considerably more fit and ready to exceed all expectations. I was a svelte 130 pounds. Ten or fifteen pounds lighter than my regular goat weight. But I could run. That was the year they brought the scrum machine that could measure impact. (Force equals mass X acceleration). Less mass equals less force. How ironic. I was taking a break and lying on a bench when the coaches came into the room and started discussing the position of hooker selection. They didn't see me on the bench and I should have probably gotten up and moved, but I didn't, I just lay there and listened to them tell each other that Helen was probably the best choice, but she simply refused to "eight-man push."

Helen and Jerri at the Women's World Cup in Spain

First, I need to tell you what a scrummage is; a scrummage is a way to restart the game after a technical infraction. It involves two pushers or props linked through their arms on either side of a middle person who is the "hooker" and hooks the ball back with their feet. These front three are supported by two individuals in the "second row," directly behind the first three, who add forward momentum to this group of five. On both sides of this linked and tight group of five are two "flankers," whose contribution to this communal push is both inward and forward (more like a squeeze). Finally, at the very back of this collection is a position appropriately called "number eight." The final forward thrust. The entire event would function like a faceoff in hockey except everyone is tied up close together, pushing forward and the referee rolls the puck down the middle of this human mass for the middle person to scoop or hook it back to their own team. To clarify even further, an "eight-man push," is where all eight of the individuals involved in the scrummage, push forward together as a singular mass of muscle and the hooker does not lift their foot to hook the ball back, thereby pushing the other team back and gaining possession of the ball by moving forward collectively

So, Helen refused to "eight-man push," *Eh?* I almost stood up and spat at them, but I didn't because good girls don't do that. At no point did anyone ever say that all they wanted from the front row was an eight-man push. They went on to say that there were several younger hookers who would likely serve them better over the long haul. Oh, Hello! I have been down this road before and I know where this is going…

And this is where Helen got off the train. What is that shit? My very favorite cliché response is the one where they say, "Don't take this personally."

Really? I spent the summer getting run off the road by logging trucks and I am not supposed to take this personally? I have sacrificed my time and my money and my career and I am not supposed to take this personally? I believed you when you told me that I wasn't good enough and that colored my entire self-view, but I am not supposed to take that personally? I'll tell you what? This is what I think...F...Y...! And you can take that personally! So, I didn't actually say that last part. But now I really wish I had. Age has a way of making you so much braver.

Needless to say, so many of my coaching philosophies developed from my experiences as a player. I always post the lineups in an environment that lets everyone accept the information in the privacy of their own emotions. I set the criteria for the selection of positions based on the opposition that we are playing and the players selected are those most suited for those skill sets on the day. I always make myself available for discussion of selection and everyone knows that I can change my mind. I try to give objective technical feedback that can be used to improve yourself. I don't have first and second teams, I have Wednesday and Saturday teams. Everyone has weaknesses, it's my job to find a way to support them and exploit their strengths. Everyone plays. Everyone starts. How long you stay on the field is up to you.

As I have grown older, I have been given the opportunity to reflect on many of my false self-beliefs. The "not good enough" file in my hard drive is full. In order to clear that file and the pain and heartache that it carries and sets off every time I get triggered by another event, I have had to go back and revisit those feelings. I have had to bring them out into the light and let myself really feel those hurts and pains. I have had to accept that it really did hurt! I have had to release them and let them go, so they can no longer affect my life. In the process of doing that, I realized that all those judgements that I felt were so unfair and so debilitating were created from my own perceptions. The coaches on the day did not have a target on my back. They did not want to hurt me. They were just doing what coaches do, picking a team. That's all. It truly wasn't anything personal…to them. It was my perspective that made it personal. And so, in the end, if we want to heal, we let it go.

Chapter 3
The Job (1988-2000)

After my baby girl, Amanda, was born in 1985, I received a call from my friend Barry Giffen. He and Gareth Jones were on the Alberta Rugby Union's board of directors and they were looking for someone to complete a government application for funding of rugby in Alberta. Would I be willing to undertake this task? It was a contract and I could set my own hours and work independently at the Alberta Rugby Union office.

There are many variables involved with having children and working. The first variable is whether or not you have to work or if there are enough resources with one income? We had just built our first home, so depending on one income was not an option. The second variable is the number of children that require daycare services. With one child, daycare is a possibility, but with two, all of your income is eaten up with the cost of daycare. I did what many moms do and decided to babysit other children in my home until my pumpkins grew a bit older. The minute Sean was school age, Amanda clarified that daycare was a much better option than hanging out with me and any other children who were invading her space. The first time I dropped her off at daycare, I returned racked with guilt at having abandoned my little blonde bundle, only to have her assert that she was not, "Weddy to go! Mommy!"

With Sean in school and Amanda happily tucked in daycare the opportunity to work at the Alberta Rugby Union office posed a wonderful opportunity. Government grant applications? High fives! I was home!

By this time, I had completed an arts degree at the University of Alberta. I was armed with the confidence of post-secondary education and I had completed my practicum at the age of sixteen. Most importantly, I was filled with the comparable inspiration and passion of a southern Baptist minister! If I had three gospel singers and a tent, I could have taken this religion on the road. My original desire to be a minister was being fulfilled with this new religion called "rugby."

Using the same protocols, I had learned as a teenager in Williams Lake, I was able to secure more government funding than the Union had ever obtained previously. Leveraging our statistics on women we doubled the eligible funding and locked women into the future of rugby in Alberta. Once the funding was approved, I hung around the office waiting for someone to tell me to go home. No one ever did, so I set off on my next great adventure.

I did take the game of rugby on the road! I travelled across Alberta introducing the game to every urban or rural school that would have me. At that time the Alberta Ballet was using a unique marketing strategy, whereby young children were exposed to ballet as an activity, creating a familiarity with the art form. The premise was that when they became adults, they would be more open to purchasing tickets to performances. I used the Alberta Ballet's strategy in terms of exposing the game to children across the province. My primary goal was to expose them to the game of rugby so that they too would be familiar enough with the game to consider buying a ticket as adults. My secondary goal was to entice them into playing the game themselves.

In the same format that my dad had taught me, I sought the advice of government sport professionals on how to build an organization that would be self-sustaining from the grassroots up. At that time, there was funding for sporting organizations to develop their sports in a three-pronged approach. The first pillar was the development and support of the grassroots game focusing on local clubs and the "access" and "participation" factor. The second pillar was the development and growth of structure that allowed for administrative and technical support to create pathways to the last pillar which was the delivery of high-performance programs. All levels involved the development and delivery of programs for players, coaches, referees, and administrators. Each pillar required planning and budgets and measurement criteria. As I had experienced previously in my life, information and advice were readily provided to those who appeared to sincerely desire and appreciate it.

Once I mastered the administration piece, I set my sights on all things technical. I realized that to truly deliver this game properly, I would require an extensive education in all of the technical components. And so, began my career in coaching development.

The Canadian Rugby Union (the national governing body), was at that point, a very lean organization involving no more than an executive director, technical director, program administrator and two secretaries. The board of directors was voted in by the member provincial union representatives and all committees were volunteer. I believe I was fortunate to be supported by the most talented group of rugby coaching mentors that has ever existed in Canada. The coaching committee' had a vision to develop Canadian coaches from the ground up. The goal was to find and develop any coach who wanted to excel in coaching rugby, whether they remained at the grassroots or sought the lofty heights of high performance. This vision aligned with my vision for Alberta rugby coaches, which was to provide the grassroots with as much development as it could handle, and to ultimately raise the level of performance for rugby players across Alberta. The National Coaching Committee was outstanding in its approach to coaches from every level of play. There was absolutely no judgment and complete dedication to the needs of every coach in every clinic. The program that they delivered allowed for the creation of Canadian careers in coaching rugby such as my own and that of my friend Ric Suggitt, perhaps the greatest coaching success story. Ric has been the only homegrown coach from the rugby outback of Alberta to coach both national teams; men and women, both games; Sevens and full Fifteens and in two countries, Canada and USA. The game of rugby is generally played with 15 players for 80 minutes. However, there is a reduced version of the game that is played by seven players for 15 minutes. Ric prided himself in being a product of that coaching committee's program, from the very bottom to the very top. The coaching committee was composed of Tom Jones, Mike Luke, Dave Docherty, Bruce Howe and Roger McEwan. They loved their work passionately, they loved rugby, they loved Canadian coaches and they loved to sing and laugh. As often as they could, they gathered coaches from the length and breadth of this country and invited them to participate in their "love affair."

Long before it was vogue with the British rugby community, these individuals were delivering a "guided discovery" model to our coaches and basing their evaluations on the coach's current and potential competencies. There was a genuine respect for those of us who did not come to the game with any background at all. The blend between guided discovery and the presentation of knowledge that we did not possess was artistically balanced. In addition to this blended approach to coach development, they encouraged us to use the inherent game information that we already possessed: Lineouts = restarts like jump balls in basketball; scrums = restarts like face offs in hockey; kick offs = starts and restarts like football; and tackling is simply mobile wrestling.

Transforming intuitive information is sometimes easier than learning a completely new game.

It has always seemed ironic to me that once this group of dedicated volunteers was disbanded, the new "Rugby Canada" brought in the "*new*" competency model for coaching delivery, complete with borrowed staff from the Rugby Football Union (RFU).[1] The delivery of this new

---

[1] RFU stands for Rugby Football Union. Ironically England is the only country that doesn't reference its own country. Generally, a national body would include the name of the country eg.

system is far from simple and requires the ongoing maintenance of each coach's competencies and their specific evaluations. It can become an administrative and fiscal nightmare. Simplicity it seems has become a lost virtue.

As I garnered all the technical coaching information I could absorb, I attended many clinics in various locations. I recall a session at the Asian Pacific Congress in Hong Kong, where the discussion surrounded the difficulty of "smaller stature" nations such as Japan, winning their line-out possession.[2] As the discussions moved around the various participants, I noticed a Polynesian gentleman from one of the Pacific Island countries pouring a brown liquid substance into cups, from what looked like an ice cream bucket and passing it around the room to the male participants. I say that like there was more than one woman in the room. No, just me. Each participant, except for myself, politely accepted the drink and dutifully drank the contents. As the conversation proceeded, it became very animated and incredible ideas like lifting the catchers to catch the ball and various other options were thrown out for discussion. In addition to all the animated conversation, the level of humor and laughter also escalated. After the session, I asked one of my friends what the liquid was and he replied, "Kava."

Australian Rugby Football Union. It has been a source of irritation throughout the history of the game.

[2] A lineout in rugby is like a jump ball in basketball, essentially a contest for possession of the ball after the ball has gone out of bounds

Apparently, this is a South Pacific drink that gets you high! It may have been the only time that I was grateful not to be included in the culture of male coaches as I was spared the experience of wandering around completely high for the rest of the afternoon.

In another coaching symposium that was being held at Maiden Head, on the outskirts of London, England, I arrived at the designated hotel and registered for my room. I proceeded to the session rooms and as I entered the main hallway a very stoic, white-haired gentleman approached me and directed me to sit in the chairs at the side of the room. I was somewhat surprised, but I concluded that the Canadian contingency had not yet arrived and that we were being shepherded into the session room as a delegation of sorts. I was correct in that the Canadian contingency had indeed not arrived at that point and when they did, they glanced at me quizzically and asked what I was doing.

"I was told to sit here," I replied indignantly.

They all looked at each other and burst into laughter. "Come on, you idiot, that's where the session recorders sit!" I wanted to find the stoic white-haired gentleman and clarify my status, but suddenly the room was full of statuesque white-haired gentlemen directly out of a scene from *My Fair Lady*, and I was quickly being left behind from the safety of my Canadian colleagues. I moved my registration name tag, identifying me as a Canadian Rugby Union delegate out of my pocket and pinned to my chest. After three introductions, I moved it from my chest to my collar. There is simply no need to present the male species with more opportunities to view female anatomy than exist naturally.

From all this very heady inclusion into the world of the coaching elite in rugby, my friends Gareth Jones, from Edmonton and Fred Kazakoff of Calgary, were easily convinced to take a trip to Hong Kong to the Asian Pacific Congress to convince those delegates to schedule their next gathering in Calgary. We were on a mission! Gareth's Welsh charm and optimism combined with Fred's grounded Canadian common sense and the daughter of Adolf Beyerle (moi) best milk salesman on the planet, could not be denied.

In conjunction with the Asian Pacific Congress, Hong Kong has traditionally hosted the best sevens tournaments in the world. The stadium is built into the side of a huge rock cliff and the roar of the crowd reverberates through the opening of the stadium doors. I stepped out of the cab and was overwhelmed by the great wave of noise. It was intoxicating and made me rush to the entrance doors, anxious that I might be missing something momentous on the field. The games hadn't even started. This was the audio sound track for the entire tournament, increasing in decibels only to express crowd appreciation for creative play or big hits.

There is a player's parade around the track prior to the start of the games. Generally, the players from the different countries display their various traditional clothing, which is a glorious array of colors and pageantry. The Canadians, not to be outdone, were trying to make the walk-in snow shoes. Snow shoes don't really work unless you are on snow. I felt a great sympathy for our players, who at best, were managing to move forward with feet splayed apart, pulling these awkward wooden attachments on their feet. Second to the referees, who were sporting seeing eye dogs and canes (this was a Monty Python type of joke to intimate that the referees were blind. They were poking fun at themselves and the player's widely held contention that they are blind and cannot see the infractions as they occur), the Canadians were the funniest group as they struggled around the track, appearing to have shit their pants.

Gareth and Fred insisted that our branding for this trade mission was going to be the Calgary Stampede's traditional white Stetson. We were there to sell Calgary, and this is what Calgary looks like! Hong Kong is possibly the most humid city I have ever encountered. Every part of my body dripped in water; hair included. Cowboy hats look good on tall swarthy men, like John Wayne. One of the reasons they look good on these men is because they never take them off. I spent the weekend with a permanent ring around my head, called "hat head." I was not singled out for any fashion shoot after I showed up at the tournament's official dinner in a formal dress, high heels and a white cowboy hat. Sales is a job that requires courage. The ability to step confidently forward looking like an idiot, convincing everyone that was your precise intention, is success.

We convinced the entire symposium to come to Calgary for the next symposium. We organized two international games to be played within a week of each other, with the symposium running inside the weeks' time frame. Calgary is a beautiful Canadian city nestled on the east side of the Rocky Mountains. Regardless of where you live in Canada, including Calgary, there will always be too much snow or not enough snow. The first game of the symposium on Wednesday provided all our visitors with their first encounter with snow and the second game on Saturday provided them with sun burns. And so, it goes.

The most memorable moment for me from the entire event occurred when Mike Luke was introducing the group to Pierre Villepreux, a charismatic and cutting-edge coach developer in France. The meeting room in the hotel was packed with every local and international rugby coach within a thousand-mile radius. The room was humming with conversations and upon the arrival of the "great one," everyone was quieted. That feat alone is worth mentioning to give you an idea of the level of expectation in the room. Mike gave a very glowing and bilingual introduction, which was a bit cheeky in Calgary at the time. The "great one" acknowledged his eager reception and was about to speak and asked Mike to turn on his video presentation. Mike is a computer guy, no problem. No problem until it doesn't work. Excruciating minutes go by as we experience "technical difficulty folks." The room starts to murmur. The "great one" starts to show signs of embarrassment and frustration; uncommon in most Frenchmen. I then hear the words that make me tremble with fear, "Helen, can you fix this?" I can hardly turn on a light switch, I have kindergarten children help me with my phone, and do I look like someone technical? *Oh God, Oh God! Where is the hotel techie?*

I approach the equipment, with prayers and promises of a life of sobriety. In a voice that is barely audible I ask, "Did you turn on the power." Mike flicks on the switch, the screen lights up with French children laughing and running and playing rugby! My body shudders in relief. The room erupts in laughter and catcalling and all I can feel is the warmth of a kind and generous universe who has my back. I quickly renege on the sobriety piece but continue to be grateful for merciful divine intervention.

The final moments of the Sunday's game saw Canada play Australia with a respectable score in front of a capacity crowd. Most importantly, as I gazed over Kingsland Rugby Park, I saw children throwing rugby balls to their dads and moms. I saw happy spectators singing songs in the stands. I saw spectators sitting on the wall of the overpass watching a sport they had never seen before. As the warm summer, sun from the west casted long shadows across a perfectly groomed emerald field, I gathered my bags, scooped up my family and headed home. There was no need to attend the dinner, my work here was done.

I want to talk about the issue of female equality. At this point in my life, that concept did not exist. At no point during my tenure as an employee of the Alberta Rugby Union, did I ever consider equality an issue. It was not an issue because the concept of equality did not exist. I was applying every trick in my dad's immigrant play book to just get into the game, so the issue of equality never even caught my attention. As a matter of fact, I used inequality as a reason to employ me. I was significantly cheaper than any male counterpart and comparable in observable outcomes. Before there can be more places at the table for women, there must be at least one. My time was spent gently moving the chairs of my male counterparts far enough apart to make room for my chair. Once I had a chair at the table, I worked very hard to ensure that no one noticed that I was there and that I was a female. I would send my suggestions and ideas out through the mouths of my male friends and they would smile at me and gratefully receive the accolades from their colleagues of ideas worthy of praise.

As time went on, I began to speak with my own voice, but never loud enough to let anyone feel threatened by my status. All the skills in political maneuvering that I had learned in my youth were perfected throughout this period of my life. I became very adept at furthering the expansion of the game for women completely supported by the many friends, whose respect I had earned over the course of time. In my zeal to ensure the inclusion of the women's game, I naively believed that all the women in the game were behind me, in support of me. I did not see the sabotage coming.

I watched a YouTube video the other day, when a professional female athlete was speaking to a graduating class. The point of her speech was the idea that women have been socialized to the idea of scarcity. We have been taught that there is only one chair at the table for women and we must fight each other to get it.

At the point where the women that I was trying to represent and promote decided that I was not worthy of their support, I concluded that I could not trust them either. Not only was I the only woman at the table, but my chair was precariously perched on a pillar that was being attacked by other women. In the 30 years of working in rugby, I have acquired three close female rugby friends. The kind that you can trust with your real self. This is not a reflection of the fine women I have worked with; it reflects my adherence to this belief in scarcity.

I am happy to say that this equality issue is under a much more revealing light currently. Not only are there many more chairs at the table, but the chairs are being firmly supported by other women who don't accept the concept of scarcity. That is the actual positive measurement of progress.

Chapter 4
And No One Says a Word
(1990-1995)

When I first started coaching, it was the most natural thing in the world for me. I felt a sincere, authentic calling to assist athletes in achieving their goals. I was surprised to find out that I possessed an ability to envision what a team might become, break down that vision into components, and then build the vision, step by step. At the very beginning, my coaching was totally intuitive because I knew so little about rugby coaching that I didn't even know how much I didn't know.

There was, however, one thing that I absolutely knew for sure. I knew that no one, not the players and certainly not the coaches, would ever say one word about what I knew or didn't know. I had learned rule number one—never, never let anyone know that you don't know—right out of the chutes as a "Johnny come lately" athlete.

For those of you too young to know what a "Johnny come lately" is, it is a late bloomer, someone who started much later than the rest. I didn't even know what rugby was until I was 23. In the world of serious athletes, that is generally retirement age. Lucky for me, the sport of rugby was also a "Johnny come lately" in Canadian sport, so we were a pretty good match. Back to rule number one: Never, never let anyone know that you don't know.

The mind boggles at how much more successful I might have been as an athlete if I had any inkling of what that coach really wanted me to do. "Helen! For God's sake, we need to have quick ball off those rucks!!!" he would scream. His command was based on his assumption that I knew what he was talking about and understood the rugby lingo. My under the breath rebuttal was based on the fact that I did not. "Well, get your pukey little scrum half (comparable to a quarter back in football) to throw the damn thing faster!"

I had no idea at the time there was a role for me in his screeching statement. Five years later, it occurred to me in one of those "*aha!*" moments, that what he had meant, was for me to stay out of the damn way and let that pukey little scrum half get to the ball quickly so that she could deliver it quickly to receiving hands. Sigh, if only that was what he had said; sigh, if only I had asked. But then he would have thought I was dumb. He would have labelled me as dumb. And I would have been that dumb hooker for the rest of my career (not entirely a stretch at that point). So just shut up and don't confirm that which you suspect they know already, and if they ask if you understand just nod, that's not technically a lie.

How fearful we are as athletes. How fearful we are as humans. How carefully we maneuver around our fears. *What if they think I am not smart enough? What if they think I am not fast enough? What if they find out that I am afraid of contact? What if they don't like me? What if they don't pick me? How will I survive the humiliation of not being good enough? I will hide in the crowd until I can figure out a survival strategy. I will not ask any questions.*

These isolated fears are so common in humans and especially within the sporting community. The ego floats to the front of our brains and starts the "what if" game. Every fear that we have as individuals and every negative thought that is hanging around the edge of the stage, boldly comes front and center and claims control of our psyche and our performance. When we manifest that fear filled outcome that has been dominating our thoughts, that same ego steps up again to reinforce its control. "I told you so!"

Quantum physics supports the notion that the energy of thought can alter matter. It becomes clear that what we think is what we create. This self-imposed isolation allows us to hide our negative self-thoughts, allows us to keep running old outdated blueprints of ourselves and most importantly it prevents us from knowing who we are and of what we are truly capable. And exactly who are we? A divine chip off the old cosmic block, a perfect being with a soul purpose. As an athlete or a coach, you are not on this field without purpose, the challenge is to figure out what exactly that purpose might be.

As a new coach, I didn't know very much but I did know that rule number one could kill you. I also knew that the players would never say a word, at least not to my face. It was only when I started to let the big secret out of the bag, nobody really knows what they are doing, that they started to trust me. At the very beginning of my coaching, I was teaching rugby to young high school girls. What a delight! We started with the "Wayne Gretzky" approach to offence:

If they want to play, they can get their own damn ball! The next step was to add the "Wayne Gretzky" approach to defense: If they steal your ball, go get it back. And, of course, the final "Wayne Gretzky" strategic approach: He shoots! He scores!

Alberta junior girl's staff at the Canmore Camp

All in all, a relatively sound strategy for the confusion on the field that was being called rugby. Because I had only recently stopped being a player, I recognized the fearful behavior of not communicating and could identify it. So, I was able to call "bullshit" on rule number one.

So, the conversation with the player would go something like this: "I know you don't know, because when I was in your situation, at your point of development, I didn't know either. I also know that you don't want to tell me that you don't know because you think that I will think that you are dumb or not smart enough or not good enough. Really, now?"

And my internal thinking would go something like this:

Really now? That would be the pot calling the kettle black! Do I look like I am in a position to judge? Let's try this new approach. How about if you tell me when you don't get what I am saying, and I will promise not to think you are dumb. But you must promise not to think that I am a crappy coach, at least until I get the hang of this. Deal!

And so, we trade off on our fears, but at least we acknowledge them. I will pick you if you will pick me. Once both coaches and athletes acknowledge that we all have these fears we can operate with a bit more honesty and clarity.

"Let's face your fear as an athlete and see if we can overcome it."

"What if I can't do this?"

"Then we will change your thinking and your vision of yourself and practice until you can.

"Together, we can move past the self-fulfilling, debilitating 'what if' statements.

"Even if you aren't who you want to be just yet, we will work until the person wearing that uniform in your dreams is the one standing in your body today."

It is somewhat amazing that in the past decade of sports development there has been a great emphasis on communication. It has become a focal point in most coaching courses. We are being taught that there must be a dedication to teaching our players to communicate. Failure to attend to this vital technical requirement will result in failure of performance. They must be able to communicate with each other on the ice, on the field, on the court, anywhere in proximity of another player. Communication is key! Ironically, apparently communication between coach and player on a personal level is not so key. If I am the coach, I don't really have to be honest with you the player. There seems to be this prevalent idea that if I can elicit a successful performance from the athlete, no other criterion needs to be met. Communication in sport doesn't seem to mean honest dialogue between the athlete and the coach. It is about the game, not the participants. So, in the context of the game it is clear we must communicate to be successful! But in the context of the bigger game—that "life" game—eh, not so much! How can this possibly work? How can I expect the player to perform if I don't know anything about how they might think or feel? How am I going to get to know them if I don't communicate? My role as the coach is not to judge whoever they are. My role as a coach is to know who they are, so that I might support them in their decisions as athletes and as people as they grow. My role is to present them with opportunities to find out who they can be and ultimately who they want to be. My role is to treat them like I would like to be treated—with open and honest communication, with empathy and love. My role is to help them find their purpose in being on this field on this day and how that might lead to knowing their ultimate purpose in being in this life.

Rule number one is different for females and males. Probably because—well, females are different from males. Shocking, I know. At first in my coaching experience, I believed that female athletes were inherently different in their approach to playing sports in general and rugby in particular. It occurred to me that they seemed somewhat more vulnerable. There was something about them that was innocent. I then realized that it was because the female athletes that I was dealing with were relatively recent participants to the sport of rugby and in some cases to sport in general. They weren't aware of rule number one. They hadn't yet experienced the repercussions of telling a coach the truth or at least their truth. The male athletes, on the other hand, had generally been involved with sport since the age of five or six and were clearly experienced in the art of "handling the coach." Each of them had learned that what a coach says and what a coach does can be two very different things. Best policy is to keep your mouth shut, work hard and hope that what you do is what the coach wants. As I progressed to higher levels of performance, the silence became more prevalent. As athletes, they had much more to lose if the coach had any indication that their understanding was even slightly questionable. At the high-performance level, there is no difference between genders. The rules of survival are deeply entrenched and the idea that anyone in the management realm has the athlete's true, best interests at heart is the stuff of fairy tales. It's the team. There is no "I" in team remember? In some cases, there is no "us" either. It's all about the best interests of the team, which coincidentally generally reflect directly the best interests of the coach. Funny how that works. Apparently, the coach always knows best!

If you think that rule number one is exclusive to athletes, you are wrong. I attended my first coaching clinic with a fist full of questions and a naive belief that this would be the solution to my dilemma. I thought I was going to be in an environment of learning and growth and sharing of wisdom and knowledge. When the New Zealand national team coach and strategic guru politely asked, "Any questions?" I let fly.

"Well what about body positioning? How do I get them to change pace.in fact what exactly do you mean when you say that? Does that mean we all run slow and then fast or does it mean you run slowly and then I run fast? What about lineouts? How do I win lineouts with short players?"

Apparently "any questions?" is in fact a rhetorical question. But I didn't know that, and I didn't have just one question! I have five million questions! There was a great deal of uncomfortable shuffling. Heads started moving together with quiet comments going from ear to ear. A great deal of nodding was occurring throughout the room. I stopped long enough to hear an increase in the collective group murmur. It was the first time I really felt like the only woman in the room. Apparently now is not the time for those questions and notice how no one else is asking any of those questions. Good point. "Am I the only one who doesn't know this stuff? Apparently if the rest of them don't know, they aren't telling, or asking. *Unhuhhhhk*...back to rule number one, never let anyone know you don't know.

I have never quite understood why, as coaches, we are determined to operate in total isolation. It just seems so ineffective to me. Here we are, finally at a point where we can call the shots and we don't want to ask anyone to tell us anything because we are afraid that they might find out we don't know everything, or as in my case, anything. I am thinking that they will likely be able to find out the big secret once they see the bad performance of the team.

But what if the team performs well? What if we win because the players are pretty good? Well, now I can't talk to the players either, because what if they find out that it wasn't my coaching? What if the players know more than I do? Can someone tell me why that is a bad thing? Why am I supposed to know more than everyone? About everything? Well, clearly, I will be better off if I just listen, pretend to know everything I need to know, and not let anyone know that there is stuff I don't know.

The only problem with that approach is that there is a great deal of anxiety that comes from all that self-doubt. It didn't take a psychology degree to figure that one out.

"I'm not sure that I know enough. I am also not sure that I know more than the players, add to that the idea that the coach is supposed to know more than the players and a really good coach knows more than most of the other coaches. Yikes! I am in big trouble. Well, actually I am in big kaka because I'm not supposed to let anyone know that I don't know, which is usually how you go about learning more of this stuff."

What a Catch-22. What a silly circle this is! How ridiculous is living in fear of everyone finding out that you don't know what you think. They think. You should know! There is absolutely nothing logical about that and certainly nothing that is going to make you want to do this coaching thing for very long. It is set up to fail. A coach operating from fear is not likely to find that experience fun or rewarding. Here it is again, ego pushing the fear agenda, all the "what ifs," all the self-doubt, all those criteria based on what everyone else thinks and nothing based on what I feel.

The irony is that once we have collected a body of information and experience and we are at the point where we know some things, we still don't want to tell anyone anything, because now we don't want them to know. Amazing, since all that we know will be revealed and exposed the minute we take the field and actually "show" everyone.

I used to attend coaching clinics and wonder if everyone was lying. There were always successful coaches who appeared to be sharing their secrets for success for all the other coaches to review and discuss. I remember attending a coaching clinic and being totally confused by this technical piece of information that was being hailed as the latest, greatest technique. I just couldn't seem to grasp how it worked. I kept asking what seemed like redundant questions to the point where the facilitator encouraged the group to "move on to keep on schedule." A kindhearted older coach, with obviously nothing to lose, leaned over to tell me that the "teaching" coach never tells the group the entire technique. That would be stupid. Other coaches would then know how to counter this successful technique. Silly girl! So, tell me why I just paid $400.00 to attend a clinic that is only going to provide me with 85 percent of the information I need just because some day I might be coaching against the "successful coach?" Trust me, by that time, there will be ten different techniques that have hit the "play of the month list," and the "successful" coach will be long gone dead!

It finally occurred to me that the only positive aspect of this coaching environment was that it was ripe for a new approach. I started simply saying things like: "I don't know, what do you think?" Well, guess what? Turns out this is a generally accepted teaching practice called "guided discovery." Well. except for the "I don't know" part. Apparently, teachers really do know.

Really? And how do we know that they know? Here we go again. Never mind, I am OK with the guided discovery method particularly if I am also being guided at the same time. Once I actually told the players that I didn't know everything, but I knew some things and more importantly I had a very strong intuition about some other things, my anxiety levels dropped significantly! I now had the freedom to ask them what they thought was happening on the field and they had the freedom to tell me. All that exchange of information free from judgment, now that is effective communication. I also learned that the "Gretzky" method of coaching was not a bad way to go. Do the simple things really well so that you can do them under pressure, get possession, keep possession, when you lose possession attack them, so you can regain possession and then score. When the game is about the performance of your athletes and not your performance, it can be the most fun on the planet!

When I first started writing this book, this was the end of this chapter, or rather the end of this "rant." I talked to my rugby colleagues complaining that I had believed I had so much to say, but sadly when the pen hit the paper it seemed so much less than all the emotion that had propelled it to this point. I believe now that the reason I stopped writing was because I was fearful that if I said exactly what I thought, I would, at the very least, be scoffed at and most certainly ridiculed. You see the reason I first started to coach was the most sincere and noble of human attributes. I wanted to contribute to the development of young athletes. I wanted to help young people understand themselves more clearly and their relationship to the rest of the world through this environment of sport. I wanted to help them achieve their goals. I wanted to help them realize the potential that I saw in ALL of them. I wanted to help them learn that failure, according to the world as it has been presented to them, does not necessarily mean failure in a personal context. There are no mistakes! Failure is an opportunity to review, contemplate and learn. It doesn't need to be the big bad thing that the world has taught us. Failure as a verb doesn't translate to failure as a noun. We can fail forward! Failure can help us to advance. I wanted to help them be fulfilled and purposeful human beings. I believe that sport is a wonderful medium to show them how wonderful they are individually and how incredibly wonderful we could all be together, as a community.

I was so lucky in my playing experience with rugby. I happened into a sport that was inclusive. Too many players? Simple—make more teams! Too short and fat? Simple—your position is hooker or prop (pushers and lifters)! Too skinny and small? Simple—you are on the wing (runners)! Too aggressive? Simple—you can play flanker (tacklers)! That's right—everyone plays! There is no cutting in rugby! Well, at least that's how it was when I started. This game embraced a culture of family. Each club had its own black sheep and they watched over them and kept them in line. Each club had its elders and there was a tradition of respect allocated there. Each club had its stars and its worker bees, and each was given recognition for their valued contribution. When I was introduced to this game, there was a tradition of "paying it forward" and respecting your opposition. Youth was the most important aspect of each club. There was only one referee amongst 30 players and they were and still are the "*keepers*" of the game. When the game was over, it was over. Everyone acknowledged their own survival and respected the contest itself. Beers for all! Buy your opposite number—the player on the opposing team who sports the same number as you do—a beer to recognize your appreciation of their efforts and indeed their survival or dominance. In earlier days, teams even sat down to share a meal after the game. This was my experience. This game and the community that provided it to me, allowed me to *belong*. They encouraged me to shine and picked me up and dusted me off when I fell into the many ruts along the road. They guided me as a player and a human. They taught me tolerance and fairness in conjunction with competition. They taught me to laugh and work hard. They taught me to be generous and fearless. They taught me balance and humility. They taught me to excel personally by working for the greater good of the entire community. I am sure this confession may evoke a knowing sigh from elders in the community and a snort of condemnation from those far removed from all this emotional awareness. Who knows, maybe I'm wrong, maybe anyone who has been saved by a sport will know who they are and agree that it was the one place that they could be free of the world and feel good and valuable, long after their "best before date" had expired.

So that was why I wanted to coach. I wanted all those players to experience the same growth and positive development that I did. I wanted everyone who crossed my path and experienced my coaching to leave my team a more evolved human being, and most importantly, to feel the need to "pay it forward."

The key to helping anyone achieve anything is to love them unconditionally, without judgment or expectation. That's right, I said the "L" word. It is clear to me that you must love people if you want to coach. Why else would you want to do this? If you don't love kids, you shouldn't teach. Why would you? If you don't love people, you should not coach. It is not natural to want to help anyone achieve anything if you don't have the capacity to love them. At this point, I would surmise that all the coaching courses you may have taken in your life have addressed the technical, the strategic and any means available to help you be successful. Translation? Winning. It is my contention that the greatest gift that coaching provides, both to the participant and the coach, is the opportunity to love people and help them feel good about who they are and what they are doing. This cannot occur in an environment of judgment and fear. This cannot occur if we are afraid to communicate with honesty.

It becomes apparent to me now that "rule number one" is a coach's first challenge. My suggestion is to rescind rule number one. If you are coaching from an authentic motivation, the desire is to help players realize their potential as players and people, and to get rid of the judgment and the fear. Allow the players to communicate honestly and listen to them, not to your own ego. Hear their words. Hear their fears. Hear their self-judgments and self-beliefs based on their fears. Empathize. Remember when you experienced the same feelings. Guide them to a place where they can be heard and then help them to learn to listen. Almost everyone is terrified of failing. In their frantic justification of all their failed actions they can't hear you tell them, "It's OK."

Their own egos are beating them up so badly they can't hear you gently tell them you believe in them. They are safe. They are safe being exactly who they are at this moment and they are safe at whatever level of performance they are at right now. You may have to help them change their beliefs about themselves to allow them to find their potential. Of course, the same applies to you. You may also have to change your self-belief to allow yourself to reach your potential as an effective coach.

When we were very young children, we were perfect beings. We had no limitations and we were not aware of anything we could not achieve. The world has convinced us that we are "not good enough." Our job as coaches is to dispel that myth, both for ourselves and our athletes. We must find our authentic selves. I believe that to be authentic you must be vulnerable. Take that fear that your ego and everyone else's ego has created in you and kick it to the curb. Being authentic is being courageous. Speak to your players the same way that you want them to speak to you. Love them unconditionally as human beings. Accept the players for who they are, not for who you want them to be. Allow them the safety and freedom to be vulnerable. Allow them to be their authentic selves, even with all the baggage they might be carrying. The energy that you give to them is the energy that that will bounce right back to you.

We are all different. We all have different styles of delivery. There is a great deal of research to support that different players will respond positively to a varied array of different coaches. Human beings, on the other hand, can generally feel when another human being is authentic or simply following an ego-driven motivation. Not all players will be motivated by you. Not all players will respond to your delivery. Most players will recognize your authenticity. Most players will respond to honest communication. Some players will find their potential in an environment free of fear, supported by a coach who is free of judgment and provides unconditional love to all the people in their sphere of influence. If that can happen with your players, it can certainly happen with your colleagues. Positive energy begets positive energy. Say goodbye to rule number one.

Chapter 5
Becoming Part of the Clan

As I reflect on the issue of authenticity in coaching, I am reminded of one of the most enjoyable seasons I have ever experienced. Most rugby clubs provide three levels of competition for their adult participants. The first team is usually a collection of the most aspiring players whose skills and experience allow them to play in the most competitive level of club competition. The second team is a collection of players who are generally serious about their performance, however, lacking the development and experience required to be performing at a first-team level. The third team is generally a mix of younger players entering into adult competition and older players moving away from the commitment and physicality of the higher levels of competition. Most coaching sessions involve at least 30 to 40 players. Most clubs require at least one head coach and optimally, two assistant coaches.

My friend Ric Suggitt was coaching the Clansmen Rugby Football Club. The club was created by one of my favorite people on the planet, Dave Graham, a Scotsman, who possessed a sword like wit and a sarcastic sense of humor that would have tickled even Oscar Wilde. The

Clansmen was a club renowned for its masculinity and bravado. Scottish national hero, Sir William Wallace, would have been truly proud of this crew.

Ric had asked me to come and help him coach the second team. I had recently completed my duties with an opposing team, the Druids, who had not renewed my term as their coach. The club was close to my home and I loved coaching with Ric. So why not? I arrived at the clubhouse on a bright blue-sky Monday evening and Dave, bless his heart, asked me if I had come to toast the ensuing season with him. "No," I replied, "I have come to coach the seconds."

"The seconds?" he said, as he choked slightly on the swallow of brown ale now following its course down the wind pipe instead of the esophagus. "The seconds?" he again questioned, clearing his throat.

I looked at Dave quizzically. "Yes, the seconds," I replied in the most affirmative manner.

"Well, then," he said, gazing out to the field with a small twitching smile forming on his lips.

"Well then," I retorted. "I'd better get at it."

I marched off the deck of the club house and headed across the sea of green, manicured grass to the middle of the field. When Moses parted the sea, I can only imagine that the waves moved in the same manner the Clansmen rugby players parted as I walked toward the center of the field where Ric was standing. My friend Ric has never held a great respect for tradition and was clearly enjoying this moment of realization for his players. Not only was I a female, but I was the female who had coached the opposition who had defeated them in the previous season.

"Most of you know Helen," he said, "She is going to help me coach the seconds this year."

I am not sure if Ric's elongated pause was for effect or if he was waiting for some type of response. An hour passed in the space of those few seconds of silence. No one moved. No one spoke. Male faces trying to contain their abject disbelief. I stood in the middle of this circle of male dominance, the object of curiosity, disbelief, shock and finally disgruntled acceptance.

The Clansmen seconds were a collection of young football players who had been introduced to rugby through Ric's previous involvement in football. They were all between the ages of eighteen and twenty-three. Old enough to drink and have babies but too young to consider the consequence of either. In typical football format, they all had nicknames reflecting their various prowesses. My friend Ric was called "Sluggo," reflecting his running style. Chocolate Rocket was a young black man with amazing speed. "Chopper" was a barrel-chested front row forward (aka lineman in football) known for his love of motorcycles and crunching tackles. Together, we were the most eclectic collection of personalities, abilities, and migrant souls. The one common denominator we found was that we all had an overpowering desire to laugh and have fun. Being authentic was a requirement because this group of young men with absolutely no sense of social pretense would locate and devour any frailty or sensitivity shown.

"Helen, you seem a bit tense and somewhat testy. Are you in menarche?" Howling, juvenile, authentically delicious laughter at my expense, showing me their knowledge of the new word. Get mad? What for? Be offended? Why? Appreciate their ridiculous, innocent boy type humor and laugh? Why not? Their non-judgmental, unaffected laughter was somehow contagious.

And so, we proceeded to train and play. There are many times when coaching turns out to be more about understanding your players and what they can and want to do, rather than what you want them to do. It became abundantly clear to me that this group of delightful, talented, testosterone-laden young men were motivated by a singular drive—and that was to have fun! The standard motivations that applied to most athletes involved in sport simply did not apply to this group.

We need to practice developing our skill level. No, we don't. We are already fabulous. OK, how about we need to practice preparing ourselves for the opposition? No, we can beat anyone. Hummmmm. OK, how about this one? We need to practice filling these two hours with fun? Yeah! Helen, you are the best coach we ever had! Would you consider having sex with your players? No? OK, what are we going to play?

And so, the summer progressed. The training sessions were the most creatively planned training sessions that I have ever put in front of a group of players. The longest any drill could last was eight minutes. The skills derived from that drill had to be tested in a game situation for a minimum of 10 minutes. Unit drills could only last 20 minutes and again had to be transformed into a game setting for a minimum of 10 minutes. Verbal description of the proposed strategy for the upcoming game could only last five minutes. Anything longer than that would cause unfocused eyes to glaze over. Team practice involving that same strategy could only last as long as it took them to execute (without opposition) five times consecutively. At that point, according to this group of self-appreciating players, they were ready. We won games and we lost games. The most wondrous thing about this team was their sheer delight and joy in simply playing. They caught the ball, they laughed. They dropped the ball, they laughed. They made herculean tackles, they laughed. They got pounded into the ground, they laughed. They lost, and they laughed at how badly they played. They won, and they laughed at how wonderfully they played. I was me and they were them. There was simply no need for anyone to be anything more than who we were. In hindsight, that season was a season of coaching nirvana. Only I didn't realize it at the time.

We made our way to the final of the regional competition that year. Our strategy was quite simple. Since we had all kinds of football skills and not very many rugby skills, we focused on the former. The ball in our hands was a bit of a liability, but we could kick the eyes out of sparrows, run like the wind, and tackle like demons. We proceeded to kick the ball to the opposition and put the onus on them to create some type of offence with us descending upon them like the plague and devouring their receivers like a pack of wolves. It was easier for us to make them drop the ball than to carry it ourselves. It was an easy run to the try line after picking up a dropped ball behind their line of defense. It worked. They all agreed it worked. Then we arrived at the final game.

The universe it seems has a sense of irony if not humor. I was coaching the Clan 2nd division team against the Druids 2nd division team, which was the club that I had coached the previous year, when we had defeated the Clan. I was confident that our strategy would prove successful against this team. All season long, I had rolled along with this collection of joyful souls not caring a great deal about the outcome and laughing with them at our seemingly uncharacteristic success.

Today was different. Today my ego came to the game with me. Today, I wanted to show that Druid club what they gave up when it chose not to have me coach the year following the success of winning the regional championship. I had heard via the players that at the end of the season, many of the Druid club leaders wanted to obtain the services of a "real coach," not some woman. Today I had a score to settle. It was one of those classic late sunny Saturday afternoons in the Alberta Indian summer. It was perfectly warm with a slight breeze. The fields at Ellerslie Rugby Park were perfectly manicured and emerald green. Greens were four inches high on the playing surface, allowing a cushion for tackling and high enough to keep the ball from bouncing out of the playing field. The perimeter lines were cut lower to the ground highlighting a crisp and decisive white boundary. The scoreboard had recently been painted to clearly indicate "home" and "away" teams. The field had been roped and the teams allocated their places on opposite sides of the field. We were on the west side of the field, closest to the spectator stands. I had on my professional coaching attire: Clan golf shirt, matching shorts, Rugby Canada baseball hat, socks and running shoes and, of course, the appropriate "you can't see what I'm thinking" sun glasses. My hair was pulled back into the appropriate genderless pony tail. I was a professional. I was equal to the task. I was ready. It was all in place, the strategy, the preparation, the team. There was nothing left to chance. I was in complete control.

Every coach has a specialty "thing" that provides them with a trademark for their particular style of coaching. My "thing" is the pregame talk. I spend nights lying awake thinking about creative expressions to inspire, to ignite, to move those players to the level of excitement that promotes their best performance. I should have known that when I finished my pregame talk to my weird, wonderful group of goofballs and added, "Whatever you do, don't run the ball out of our own end," they would accept the challenge. And they did. Rather than kick the eyes out of sparrows, they showed me how they could in fact string three passes together—under pressure, intense pressure. OK. maybe not that time, but for sure the next time! At half-time, this collection of athletic free spirits met Helen, the authoritative, domineering and somewhat abusive but certainly seriously playing for all the marbles, coach.

"What are you doing?"

"All season we have worked on and perfected this style of play!"

"Suddenly you think you can pass and catch?

"Suddenly you want to pit your skills against the big boys?

"Play to our strengths! Use the strategy that got us here!

"*Do what I told you to do!*"

I could not have done anything more counterproductive. With their egos now front and center, there was little room for joy or frivolity. They now needed to show themselves and me that they were in fact as good as any other team and certainly good enough to run this ball and any ball from theirs or any other end of the field.

When your ego is running the show, you can be assured that every little piece of your personality that you keep under the covers on most days, will come rushing forward with the same exuberance as the puppy escaping through the front door. Hello! Here I am! You have been hiding me for quite some time now, but I am free now to pee and poop anywhere I please!

After the fifth time that we tried to run the ball out of our defensive area instead of kicking, and were pinned down and scored upon, I lost my temper. I kicked the water bottles sitting by our bench at the side of the field. The west side of the field. The side closest to the stands. I kicked them with such ferocity that one of the bottles hit a small older woman in the stands. She was one of the Druid's grandmothers. Of course! She was there watching her grandson, frail, tiny and innocent. Of course! Not impressive, Helen. As a matter of fact, that's pathetic! The Druid's are glad now that they didn't ask some loose cannon like you to coach them again. Vindication for them! Embarrassment for you! The best made plans. Sigh! At the end of the game it was Helen and her ego—zero, Druids—way more than the Clan.

In the end it was that same ridiculous Clan second team laughter that brought me back to reality. When the players saw that I had nailed an old lady in the head with a water bottle because of the frustration, I was experiencing coaching them, they exploded with that same howling, juvenile, authentically delicious laughter at my expense. Humility is a friend of mine. Humility loves me and hangs around to provide me abundant opportunities to learn the precise definition of the word. In learning those lessons of humility, I also learned forgiveness. Mostly I had to learn to forgive myself and love myself enough to be able to laugh as freely as the goofballs that I was coaching. We were, if nothing else, totally authentic and they loved me in the same non-judgmental, innocent way they loved the game. I was blessed to learn so many life lessons with such a group of true free spirits.

The score indicated that we had lost the game but I can assure you that not one of those Clan players thought they had failed. The idea that they might be failures based on the outcome of that event did not even cross their minds. They left the field solid in the conviction of their own greatness and mildly surprised at the prowess of their opposition.

Chapter 6
It Isn't About the Outcome, It's About the Performance (1989–2004)

Being human presents many lessons over the course of your time here on "Boot Camp Earth." There is a big fat primary lesson that captures many people for long periods of time. It is a lesson that many people never really quite learn until their time starts to diminish. The big fat lesson is that, you may want to think you have the big "C" word under wraps, but you don't. Many of us have spent lifetimes trying to gain, have and maintain "control," but the bottom line is that you can't, don't, and won't ever have control of the world around you. The universe is not designed that way. It is designed to keep changing, and sending through lessons that you need to learn. Many people have become obsessed with being in control. In order to believe that they are in control of their world, they have invested lifetimes seeking knowledge, organizing their environments, and building systems that support the idea that they can control of outcomes. When it becomes painfully obvious that all that effort has not provided them the success they are seeking, they speak of probability and odds. They defer to the idea that if they cannot be in absolute control, they can at the very least organize the odds to be in their favor.

That effort and work seem to me to be the biggest waste of time and generally not very much fun. I am going to give it up right here. I, Helen Wright, do not have control of my world, your world, or anyone's world.

So, why would I think for one moment that I could map out and plan a strategy that will always be successful in beating every other team that I play? Now, I am not saying you should not plan or be crazy creative in your plan to beat the opposition, I am just saying don't hang your hat on the outcome because you can't actually control the outcome. The weather is out of your realm in terms of control. In many cases the competitive environment is out of your control.

There has been a great deal of time and effort dedicated to ensuring that the athlete is comfortable in the environment in which they are going to perform. All this work has gone into ensuring maximum performance. It has been my experience that the referee is also generally a complete wild card. History has proven throughout the ages that there will always be opposing teams that are better than yours, and many who are not better will still beat your team. So, if we can logically conclude that you cannot control the outcome, why do we place so much emphasis on it? Well, first off, winning is fun! Secondly, winning provides us with credibility and perhaps notoriety, and who doesn't like attention? And if we are really lucky, winning might actually have some tangible rewards, like money.

So, I agree: Winning feels good; I like winning. But if winning is good, then does that mean losing is bad? Perhaps so bad that I could be motivated not by how much I like winning, but rather by how much I hate losing? Remembering that I don't have any control over the world, that can be a pretty desperate place to be coaching from. As a coach, it can move you from one end of the spectrum to the other—the joy of winning to the fear of losing. That complete reversal in motivation can happen to the best-intentioned coach without their ever realizing it.

What if we turned it all around? What if we actually took on a more philosophical approach? Maybe if we spent our time teaching and creating excellence in performance, we might find the whole endeavor so much more satisfying. If we actually took the time to teach the skills required to make the best decisions. What if we honed these skills to a degree that they could be performed almost subconsciously, allowing the conscious mind to attend to the details and decisions of where and when. What if we taught decision-making without the fear of making the wrong one? What if there was no such thing as a wrong decision, just an opportunity to make a better one. That truly is playing the odds. The more perfectly we play, the more chances we have of scoring and defending, and the more likely it is that we may experience a positive outcome. What if we appreciated the sheer quality of the performance more than the outcome of the game? Many of us have experienced watching a game of such a high-caliber that our delight with the excellent performance far surpassed the concern of the outcome. Clearly, losing in those circumstances was simply destiny.

The world of sport has become impatient with human beings. The world of sport has determined that if it cuts to the chase right away by just picking the biggest, the fastest, the most talented, and heading toward the goal of winning, no time will be wasted. We don't seem to have the time to invest in the refinement of skill or the development of the craft. This seems such a loss of opportunity. The athlete loses the opportunity to experience the quiet confidence that comes with knowing how to execute expertly. The athletes lose the opportunity to play intuitively and creatively with each other. The coach loses the opportunity to see that most rewarding of all looks—the one that says: "Wow—look what I did! It worked! Thank you!" But perhaps the biggest problem is that is everyone loses the "art" of sport. Not only is the beauty of creative performance lost, but also the joy of contesting it. Our imaginations are lit up when we are witness to true creativity in sport. It excites us to see performances where skills, both individual and team, allow for spontaneous creativity. The magic of that moment takes our breath away! And yet when we coach, we seem reluctant to invest the time or energy to teach and encourage our athletes to pursue excellence in their performance. We are clear in our instructions: Do not deviate from the game plan and do not take any chances. We are in such a hurry. We need to win. We need to be successful.

That is how success is measured in our world—by wins. We have forgotten that the joy of playing the game for athletes is having the confidence and the ability to, on occasion when the spirit moves us, take a chance and create something extraordinary. Even if the outcome is not successful, the performance was brilliant!

Several years ago, Lance Armstrong wrote a book called "It's not about the bike." Ironically, we have since learned that it wasn't about the race either. It was about winning the race at all costs.

I suggest that it is also not about the game. It is about the performance. When we agree that it is about the performance, we can let go of the win-versus-loss mentality. It becomes more of a progression, a development of both the athletes and the team. This becomes an entirely different environment within which to work. It now promotes the idea of skill development, individually, in units, and as a team. It is possible for your team to have its absolute best performance and lose the game. Likewise, a team can underperform and win. If the criterion for the standard of performance is created within the team then the opposition makes no difference. If the unit goal is to win 70% possession of all of the ball restarts, then the fact you are playing a more accomplished opposition has no bearing on the desired outcome. We want to perform well enough to come away with 70% of the possession from those opportunities. The totally cool part of coaching is that we can now be creative about how we can achieve that.

Now, the fun part of playing this human chess game is introduced. Strategy! I love strategy. I especially love it when the players are involved in its creation. It has been my experience that players love strategy as well! This is the absolutely most fun part of sport. We spy on the opposition, collect their information, make a sneaky plan to enhance our performance, and then roll it out there on the battle field. Your team makes the first move, engaging the front line in hand-to-hand combat. But my team has moved the location of the battle. Now if we can perform our skills better than you, we have an open point of penetration. A hole and a possibility to penetrate your defense and score! And so, it goes! One encounter after another, one opportunity after another, one performance after another until the time is up and someone counts the score. We evaluate our strategy. We measure our performance. And we pump our fists in triumph or we create a new resolve, but most importantly we look forward to the joy of performing again! If we are lucky athletes, there is someone on the sideline—a coach or team of coaches—who has watched us perform, who has collected the information, the feedback, and who is excited about helping us continue to improve our performance. That someone is a coach who is engaged in our journey down this path and who sees how valuable this endeavor is, especially to us.

In 1988, after having been selected to the first National Canadian Women's Rugby team and participating in the first international test match against the American team, I retired as a player. By this time, I had played for eleven years and had my two children, Sean and Amanda. After Amanda was born, a friend of mine, Barry Giffen, called and asked if I would be interested in working for the Alberta Rugby Union. As I mentioned in previous chapters, these were early days for women's rugby in Canada, so all things were possible. Sometimes the parallels between the growth of a human and the growth of an institution are astounding. When you are that young and innocent, you simply don't realize that there are any limitations. You are so focused on the direction of your greatest visions that everything is just another opportunity to grow. Just like children, we want to be grown up as fast as we can. Just like children, when we become older and conditioned, we look back with longing to a time of pure joy and creativity.

I began working at the Alberta Rugby Union with an unstoppable passion and a clear vision to save the world. I believed with complete conviction that sport in general and this sport in particular could allow children, men, and women to find their spirits, their souls. I believed that the community of sport could provide the environment for collective goodwill and human growth. I took every coaching course that was available. I sought every piece of information that could help me convince the rest of the world that sport was the answer we were all looking for. I captured the support of the Canadian Rugby Union's National Coaching Committee (a group of elite coaches in Canada charged with the mission of developing rugby coaches in this country). They could hardly believe that I was for real. I worked relentlessly to deliver the game to the backwoods of Alberta. I recruited two young coaches who shared my passion. Rick Suggit and Dave Hill became the "apostles" of rugby in Alberta, taking the message to the hinterland.

There is one particular event stored in my memory bank that I know will provide me with this warm and rewarding feeling well into my old age. It is a moment that shows how sport can bring out the best in all of us.

Rick and Dave were on the road continually providing schools with "outreach clinics." These were introductory physical education classes that taught kids how to play rugby and the accompanying principles of the sport. Ric was asked by Cheryl Dawes, one of the teachers who was an avid rugby supporter, to come to a school in Spruce

Grove, a short distance from Edmonton. The day had progressed in a fairly routine fashion. One class right after the other, with children running and playing, learning to play rugby with that frenetic chaos that accompanies breathless laughter. In the last class of the day, the children bubbled out of the school and onto the field full of noise and energy. Mixed in the middle of this hobbit sized mass of bodies was a face complete with anticipation and a beaming smile. The little upturned nose and close-set eyes gave away the down syndrome condition of this eager pint-sized participant. The teacher, trying to catch up with her cheering charges intended to assist the little pumpkin to the side of the field where it might be somewhat safer. Before the teacher realized what was happening, Ric had the little boy by the hand and swung him up onto his shoulders. He began running around the field laughing and providing play by play to the rest of the class about the decimation about to occur if he and his high riding colleague made contact with any of them. The field was full of children running madly about squealing in delight as Ric and his little high-flying cherub chased them. The teacher called me the next day to let me know that the little fellow's mom told her he hadn't stop grinning until he fell asleep that night. I am not sure which picture I cherish the most—the bright shining eyes and huge smile on the face of that little boy, or the equally delighted smiles on the faces of all the other children.

Experiences such as this simply fueled my passion to a greater degree. I remember one coaching "super clinic," where I was so high on my vision that I convinced my colleagues that if I had three gospel singers and a big tent, I could take this religion on the road!

We had coaching clinics that brought in the very best coaches of the time. We had international matches that allowed children to mingle with these huge rugby superstars. We had organized an international match between Canada and Scotland. I received a call from a teacher from Williams Lake, B.C., which was my tiny hometown in the interior. He indicated that he was bringing his high school team on a field trip and would he be able to have the kids obtain autographs after the game. Williams Lake is a taxing ten-hour drive from Edmonton. I was so moved that this coach was going to this length to provide this opportunity to his players that I promised him not only would they have that access, but they could attend the Scottish team's practice as well. After the main event, the coach approached me to thank me for this incredible opportunity. Apparently, not only had the Scottish management introduced the boys to the team, but the Scottish players had gone out of their way to include these young players in their practice as well. Each of these young players was going home with their own dreams of playing on their own national team. When I grew up in Williams Lake, I don't even remember a game called rugby. This small remote town in the middle of cattle and timber country has now produced some of the finest national rugby players in Canada. That is not by accident. It is a direct reflection of the dedicated vision of those coaches who see the same opportunities in sport and rugby that I do.

One interesting side note regarding all the events we organized to share our love of rugby to young people is that we never lost any money. We always broke even financially. Those who could donate funds. Those who couldn't, donated time and effort. I guess the reason it was possible was because everyone from the president of the national union, the provincial union, the regional union right down to the facility folks, had decided that this was worth doing. They believed in the value of these events. They shared the vision that exposure to this game could change lives. And who knows, it had changed their lives just as it had mine. In later years, the Canadian Rugby Union would come to scoff at the idea that goodwill and collective vision have anything to do with the professional game and the national team. Ironically, the national men's team has never reached the same level of success as it did in those more formative years, when the budget was significantly less than it is today.

During the period of time between 1982 and 1999, I coached anyone and everyone who would have me.

I coached provincial junior women, my absolute favorites. They were the most responsive group of individuals on the planet. These young women completely believed me when I told them that they were the absolute best rugby players in the country. The greatest thing about these girls was that they were big, they were small, they were smart, they were fearless, they were timid, but primarily they were this big conglomeration of talent and size and emotion. Their most important attribute was their willingness to accept my vision that they could accomplish anything. I recall being on Vancouver Island at a national championship for girls under the age of 19 in a town called Duncan. There is a great presence of aboriginal culture in this area. In typical West Coast form, the morning rainy mist had given way to a brilliant sunny afternoon. We were gathered at the local rugby fields, where the home team appeared to be exuding its confidence and dominance by running around the perimeter of the fields chanting positive self-talk slogans. I noticed the girls becoming more and more anxious. It is a daunting situation for the most experienced of athletes to enter the realm of the opposition's home turf, complete with all their usually vocal supporters. I could sense the girl's trepidation. I felt a need to heighten my protective bubble of energy. I needed to place them safely under our own team's protective dome. There we stood, under the cloak of the West Coast rain forest, shivering from nervous excitement. I began the pregame talk convincing them that they were a tribe—an Alberta tribe; a tribe in a foreign hostile environment where we would have an opportunity to create a presence unlike any presence ever presented here before. As with many aboriginal tribes, we were the only source of our own support. I spoke to them of a spiritual source that provides courage to those who go bravely into battle, that provides speed to our feet and air to our lungs when we are exhausted. I truly believe that I was so swept up in the energy of that place that I lost sight of the fact that this was really just a rugby game. In a moment of unbridled passion, I pretended to paint war paint on their faces, dipping my fingers into a bag of ice water, and then running my fingers across their faces as if stroking on paint. Some of them, lost in the moment quivered with anticipation, and some of them, much more grounded than I, giggled at the pure ridiculousness of it all. They ran onto the field completely secure in knowledge of who they were, where they came from, and the incredible potential they carried with them. I, on the other hand, gave thanks that they loved me so unconditionally that they let me keep my dignity even though I was showing signs of serious dementia. I can't remember if we won or lost, I can only remember that I really loved those girls, and I believe they could not help but love me too.

I went on to coach a junior men's club team, the Edmonton Druids. They were as new to me as I was to them. The very first practice was akin to two different species of dogs sniffing at each other. We knew we were the same species and therefore not antagonistic to each other. We just weren't sure about the pecking order. Well, the one nice thing about age is knowledge. I understood the alpha male syndrome completely and I'm fairly sure their understanding was limited to their intuition. Once we figured out that I was indeed the coach, and that the title made me the person who could extract penance for bad behavior, we were good to go. The fabulous thing about coaching young males is that once the roles have been established, the rest is so easy. Generally, the world appears a simple place for young men. What are your expectations for me? What is my reward for reaching those expectations? What are the repercussions for not reaching them? Would you consider having sex with your players? No? Just checking? This was the first group that I met that actually totally believed that they were indeed the best players on the planet. I actually did not need to instill any confidence; they came loaded with the innate belief in their own perfection. It was delightful! They had untainted spirits! I was an oddity, but certainly not an obstruction to their ordained greatness. We went on that year to win the regional championship and the provincial championship as well. I recall being disappointed that we couldn't just continue to play any opposition that presented itself. Somewhere deep inside myself, I wondered whether or not we could have won a world championship. I know, I know…reality, really? But when you are surrounded with an energy that has this undisputable belief in the possibility of anything, it takes you back to a moment you too were airborne, and when anything was possible!

Well, if that was a peak, coaching the same club's senior men was certainly a trip to the valley. Earlier I referred to the New Zealand players, who could not accept that a female was coaching a senior men's team. Well, we could expand that to the Irish players, South African, and the English players as well. The airplanes landed as the Druids' executive had imported all these overseas players to help our young Canadian players reach their potential with a level of security. The one thing that could have been more helpful to me coaching that year was not just a degree in psychology, but one that specialized in early childhood. Ironically, it was the South African player who supported my efforts to a degree that allowed us to succeed. I developed another love for this game of rugby through this experience. Here was this South African, who clearly could not even fathom the reality of a female coach. What he could fathom was a solid strategy that made sense and was presented by this odd person. His appreciation of rugby was greater than his preconceived notion of where women fit in this world. He also gave me credit for understanding and knowing who the opposition was, and where they might be vulnerable. Perhaps apartheid had expanded his vision of the world and the capacity of those in it. That was the year that winning meant nothing at all. That was the year that even though I was not aware of it, I allowed my confidence to be undermined by those outside myself. That was the year that those vicious doubts slipped into my self-beliefs without me having any idea of what had happened.

In 1999, we cajoled, maneuvered and bribed the University of Alberta to create a nationally sanctioned women's rugby program. These were times of restraint and budget reduction, not expansion. Thankfully, the people involved with sport at the University of Alberta were likeminded in their inclusive approach. We also had the support of a local reporter, Karl, who took our cause to be a personal crusade and propelled us into the pages of the local newspaper. With Karl behind us and the university looking to offset the gender tilt that football created, we slipped into the national arena of university competition.

I applied for the coaching position realizing that the university did not have funding for this program. In addition to ranting about my philosophical approach to rugby and my greatest desire to create a program that provided an experience to these players that would be life changing, I provided a formula for sustained funding from outside the university. I got the job. I'm not sure that my vision for the program was as influential in closing the deal as the self-funding.

The first thing that I did was surround myself with friends who had shared my vision of what sport should be, who and had a fabulous sense of humor. My best and truest friend Kerry, came on as the manager. My brainiac friend Maxi came on as an assistant coach. My true friends and allies from the Alberta Rugby Union, Ric and Matt came on as assistant coaches. My friend Joan, who was in charge of the physical therapists at the university ensured that our girls were cared for physically. Ian was the crusty, growly athletic director who provided me with the application process for creating a national framework for women's rugby competition within the existing national varsity competition framework. I did the paperwork and he represented the request for women's rugby to be included as a national varsity competition. In later years, we would recognize the huge impact that level of competition would provide to our national team program. It would become the corner stone to the national U23 team. The University of Alberta continued to provide us with a supporting energy and wonderful people that personified everything that we were trying to achieve, which was to create good human beings!

The Pandas Team After Winning the 2001 National Championship

Our first year was 1999. We had two months to prepare to take a team to the Canada West competition and if that was successful, on to the national championships. The team was comprised of many of the same girls I had coached on the provincial U19 team. They came fully prepared for this new experience. We had no idea what we were going to be up against and no opportunity to gather that information. The game of rugby allows for big people to play this game. Obviously, the fitter they are the more effective they are, but it isn't a requirement to play. I loved that about rugby and encouraged as many young big girls to play as I could. I called them "powerful pushing machines!" Needless to say, I had attracted a group of very strong females to this team. We continued to play by the Wayne Gretzky School of strategy and though simple in its approach it worked for us. We were able to defeat the teams in the Canada West competition and moved onto the national championships in Guelph Ontario. It was here that we were labelled as "one thousand pounds of Alberta beef." I am not sure if that was meant to be derogatory or not, but when your self-belief is "I am powerful," it turns into an affirmation that seems to be supported by everyone else too. Cool! The weather was blizzardy, the referee had never seen us play and was critical of every technique. On this day, at this time, this group of young women simply did what they were best at and pushed the other team over their own goal line. We won, but most importantly we performed to a level we had never reached before.

The Pandas Team After Winning the 2002 National Championship

From 2000 on, we attracted some incredible athletes whose skill levels were outstanding, particularly when it came to ball handling and running. It was at this time that we started including the players in the creation of the strategy. Because we never knew who we were going to be playing, nor would we likely be playing them more than once. We built our strategy around who we were and what we could do well. The players excelled in this area and concluded very early in the process that if in fact the opposition did not have possession of the ball, they couldn't really play. Females are so smart and like the running and playing with the ball, but not so fond of the chasing and tackling. OK, it's settled. Let's do that! The challenge with having the ball in your hands for that long is that you have to do something with it. Developing attacking skills and decision-making skills in players is like teaching new artists to paint. It is a creative process and it takes time and repetition and commitment to excellence. This group of over-achieving females saw the rugby field as a blank canvas and throughout the course of their university careers they painted a game of rugby that was breath taking. The result of this excellent performance was not surprisingly a collection of checks in the "win" column.

*The Pandas Team After Winning the
2003 National Championship*

In 2005, my friend at the University of Alberta, Ian Reid, decided that it was time for the community to see firsthand these incredibly successful rugby players. He bid to have the national championships in Edmonton in November. Many of you may not be familiar with climate specific to locations, but there is a reason that many people believe that Canada is the land of dog sleds. It snows, it blows, and it can be very cold in Edmonton in November. And it was!

By this time, we were a "bit of big deal" in our environment. We were approaching our fifth consecutive potential national title. Winning to this point had been a delightful outcome that resulted from a collective, committed effort to perform excellently. The philosophies that had driven the program to this point had been authentic. Almost every girl who played rugby for the University of Alberta Pandas was coaching in some high school or club junior program. Each of these players was committed to helping each other through their university studies. Everyone graduated. That may not have been a statistic that I could so proudly point to if it weren't for their absolute dedication to the well-being of each other.

The real winners in this story were the players. They created it all. They bought into the "good human beings" program and showed how effective that could be. We, the coaches, simply provided them with the environment and the opportunity to shine. Shine, they did! They went on to provide a rugby performance that showed little regard for the snow and the ice and the wind and the opposition. In front of their families and friends and a community of rugby diehards, they ran the ball like it was a balmy summer afternoon. As I watched them play and looked into their eager and happy faces, it reminded me of a time long ago when my feet had also followed my heart to another plane.

Helen and Kerry with first Alberta Junior Women's team

Chapter 7
There Is No "I" In Team

It has been a long-standing tradition in team sports to sacrifice the individuality of the athletes for the "greater good of the team." It is an expectation that all things personal are left at home. When you, the athlete, arrives at this team environment, the prime objective is to contribute to the well-being of the team.

When I was growing up, I watched the TV series *Star Trek* and recall particularly sinister group of antagonists called the "Borg." They were a robotic entity of beings who were all energetically connected to each other as part of an evil collective. Their goal was to dominate all beings in the universe and assimilate them into the collective. They would issue the statement, "We are the 'Borg,' resistance is futile, and you will be assimilated!"

Sometimes, I think that the sport's world has taken the concept of "team" in this direction.

A coach can choose the degree of compliance to this authoritarian type of philosophy. The choice is usually relative to the coach's level of confidence. The more insecure the coach, the easier it is for that coach to simply be a dictator. That approach erodes the need for accountability. Some allow athletes a great deal of latitude, particularly when the athletes are professionals who make more money than the coach. Generally speaking, the younger the athlete, the less latitude for individuality.

At the beginning of most seasons, there is a litany of rules that are described to athletes vying for acceptance onto any type of team. In some cases, in the more "athlete-centered" environments, mutual goal setting occurs. A great deal of the discussion in determining those goals centers around questions such as: How well do you want to perform this year? What do you think it will take for you to achieve your goals? Are you prepared to sacrifice to achieve these goals? How much are you prepared to sacrifice to achieve these goals?

It doesn't take a rocket scientist to determine that if you want to play on this team, it may be "yourself" you are being asked to sacrifice. Another implied standard view to which most athletes acquiesce is that they should feel lucky just to have the opportunity to abdicate their individualism or "self," because being on this team is the most important thing in life right now. If it isn't the most important thing in your life, then you are in the wrong room and you might as well clear out your locker right now. We are in this together; we are a family. Yikes! Sounds more like a cult or, at the least, a very unhealthy, controlling family.

The most disturbing thing about this philosophy is that many young athletes come from family environments that are abusive or dysfunctional in many ways. They have no concept of what a healthy functioning interacting group of humans even looks like. They believe that everyone else has a "normal" family and they are the sole exceptions. When they are exposed to this philosophy of removing the "I," they are happy to accommodate if they can be part of something that feels better than what they have been exposed to at home. They buy into the "whatever it takes" philosophy that usually accompanies the "no more I" philosophy and become ardent "family" members, assuming whatever role is required by the coach. Inadvertently, in their zeal to be part of this alternative family, they can become potential victims. It becomes even more frightening when these vulnerable young athletes adopt the new "family" in hopes of experiencing that special inclusive, loving environment and then are exploited by their coaches or teammates or worse, cut from the team, or the family. There is a plethora of resulting issues that can culminate into emotional tragedy for that athlete.

When I read Theron Fleury's book *Playing with Fire*, I cried. I cried because I remembered being a young person who so desperately wanted to be accepted into a team. Any team. At that point in my life, I was completely dependent on everything aside from myself to provide value to my existence. I needed to be on a team! I needed to find an identity that had value. I had no identity of my own. The only voice I heard was my ego, telling me how good everyone else's life was. All I could do was look into the lives of the people around me and try to measure up to everyone else's standards. From the outside, it appeared to me that being accepted on a team would make me more acceptable in the world. If I was acceptable to the world maybe I could be acceptable to me. The idea of providing my own source of self-love was a foreign and distant concept.

I also felt like crying because when my son was a young Midget AAA hockey player, I was one of the parental taxi drivers. In one of my many deliveries of 15- to 17-year-old young men to various ice rinks around the area, I overheard a conversation regarding the Sheldon Kennedy abuse story. Sheldon had been a young hockey player who had been sexually abused by his junior coach in the mid-80s when he played with the Swift Current Broncos. Somewhere far in the recesses of my vehicle there was a young voice who wondered if the abuse might not be worth the price of reaching the NHL. There was a chilling silence and I was stunned to be the only voice loudly professing the absolute rejection of that consideration.

So, the question that begs to be asked is: "Why do we have to give up our own individual personalities, our spirits, to be successful as a team?" Wouldn't it be a better situation if we as a group were able to incorporate our diverse "selves" into a unit that celebrated our differences and used those many abilities to overcome the obstacles before us? I always chuckled when professional players were being interviewed and questioned about their opinion of the antics of the opposition team's "shit disturber." In almost all cases the player would indicate that the "shit disturber" in question was the most annoying and irritating player to play against. Meanwhile, had they been on the same team, that same player would have been considered an asset.

Each of us has a spirit, a personality, and a history that accompanies us wherever we go. The goal of sport should not be to suppress who we are, but rather to blend all of our best parts into the tapestry of this particular team. I remember telling teenage girl rugby teams: "If you are a bitch, you do not need to change your personality to be on this team; you can be a bitch, as long as your bitchiness contributes to the mosaic of this team in a positive way. In conjunction with retaining your own personality, you must respect that others on this team may be quite different from you. If you can be a bitch, then your teammate who oozes sweetness is also allowed that freedom."

I often reminded these same teenage girl players that awareness and tolerance are two-way streets. The more you are aware of what you are putting out there, the more you will become aware of what you are attracting back to yourself. The more you are aware of the impact of your opinions and actions on others, the more you can choose whether you want to alter them or not. The object of our interaction with other humans is not to assimilate, but rather to learn and grow and choose our own paths.

I have spent a great deal of time and effort over the years trying to "earn respect" as a rugby coach. This "respect" that is so highly touted in our society is no different than any other situation where we as humans are seeking approval from other humans. We are looking for approval and value outside of ourselves. Ultimately, it is a hole no one else can fill. For the record, I don't believe that anyone can "earn" respect. We as athletes and coaches spend our lives trying to earn the respect of other people, who have no intention of giving that to us. We have bought into the blueprint that says that if we work hard and do the "right" things as athletes, then other athletes and coaches will have respect for us. No. No they don't have to, and they might not. The only way that we will ever receive respect from someone is if that person decides to give it to us. It is entirely their choice, not ours.

When I was coaching senior male rugby players who came from New Zealand (rugby is to New Zealand what hockey is to Canada) I was told that I would never—that's right, never—receive respect from this group of athletes. Why? Because I was a female. In hindsight, I am glad that they said so because there was nothing I could do about being female. If they had said the reason was because I wasn't knowledgeable or experienced, I would have fervently set out to ensure that I possessed absolutely every shred of knowledge and experience available to me. What a waste that would have been. This bit of news about being female was, ironically, was one of the most enlightening pieces of information that I had ever received! This information provided me with the clarity and realization that I cannot control what other people think. People will choose what they think regardless of what I do. I mulled that over for quite some time. I had invested my entire being into receiving some form of recognition for my passion, for my work, for my efforts, and these folks were telling me that no matter what I did or achieved, that was not going to happen. I had spent 20 years on this path expecting that if I worked feverishly, learned every possible technique and strategy, produced winning results, and provided an environment for athlete growth and development, surely that would yield respect. What a flash! It was perfectly logical. For whatever the reason might be, if people do not want to give you respect, they won't. There is nothing we can do to elicit or earn it, so we may as well spend our energies in a more productive manner. I needed to find an alternative source of value.

This was a pivotal point in my own personal growth; unfortunately, I didn't know it yet. At this point, I wasn't asking the question that should have been a logical progression from the "respect" question. The next question should have been: "If I know that I can't earn respect from other people, why am I depending on other people to provide me with a source of value at all?" Why am I letting perfect strangers, or even intimate friends tell me who I am and what I am worth? Why am I giving away all my power? To anyone?

All of my confidence was based on the feedback that I received from others. In hindsight, I could have saved myself a great deal of heartbreak had I paid attention to what was being presented to me. But it is how you handle the valleys that help you get to the peaks. In my case, there were several trips up and down that path lingering in my future.

Once I learned and was armed with this new information it became clear to me that we all have the choice of whether to give respect. That was my message to the female rugby players with "fast-bitch" fibers[3]. The key that unlocks the dilemma of keeping our identities and still functioning within a cohesive unit is that we must be willing to give our respect to teammates that might be entirely different from us. This provides coaches with the

---

[3] This is a play on words. It references a common physical term for fast twitch fibres, which are required in sprinters muscles. Generally, the faster twitch fibers you have, the more powerful your muscles are and the faster you are.

opportunity to address the issue of judgment and how it can be a virus that invades teams and destroys all their efforts. When we are trying to provide an environment that is free of fear and judgment, we have to acknowledge that the athletes themselves contribute to the success or demise of this intention. This is the primary lesson that sport can offer to the development of humankind. This is such an opportune environment for the learning of these lessons. If Barbie and Zena can choose to accept each other for all their attributes and frailties, and work together toward a common goal, they can be an awesome team! Imagine how that translates to the rest of their lives. Imagine if we could use sport to teach tolerance. How many coaches have been presented the opportunity to integrate players of different and sometimes opposing cultures?

In sport, homophobia has been a long-time virus. What better environment to show the equality of each player based on their performance rather than their sexual preference? When teams are united in a common purpose, challenged by an opposition and lifted to a higher aspiration, they can demonstrate the best of humanity can offer. When we allow players the safety of being whoever they are and provide an environment that shows their value to the team, we are teaching these world citizens how to accept each other and live together. Perhaps one of the greatest examples of this teamwork in rugby is the 1995 South African national team, the Springboks, who with Nelson Mandela's inspiration and urging, used the game of rugby to inspire themselves and an entire nation to unite in spirit to beat the world and win the world cup.

"This is not a democracy! I am the coach, and if you cannot follow my direction then you are on the wrong team. That statement could be translated to read: "This is a dictatorship! I am the king and you will obey, or I will kill you." Oh wow. Can I play on your team? Not likely. The problem in sport is that in many cases the athlete is not choosing the team, or the coach based on what might be a good experience. This team is a stepping stone to the goal, or in professional sports, the one you have been traded or sold to. This may not be a "choice" situation. It always surprises me when athletes are interviewed, and they express that the clearly dictatorial coach is easier to perform for because "at least you know where you stand." It is much more difficulty to perform for a coach who is manipulative and deceptive. What a sad commentary on coaching. What form of abuse do you prefer? I want to be clear that I know there are many very good, ethical, and moral coaches who have positively influenced the lives of many young people and continue to do so. I applaud them, and I am grateful to have been exposed to some of them. My point is that coaching is not being presented or delivered as an opportunity for the development of good human beings; it is being presented as an opportunity for the development of "winners." But what about the participants who are not the winners? We are talking about all those people participating who do not *win*. That would be 50% of all those participating in any competition at any time. If the value of coaching is being defined by the outcome as opposed to the experience, then aren't we eliminating the opportunity to positively affect the lives of 50% of all participants?

The good news relative to this type of sport is that there is a new generation of athletes who are buoyed with the confidence of having fun! The word is getting out there that if it isn't fun, they will simply do something else. Some parents are teaching their children that the quality of the experience is more important than the outcome. More parents need to teach their children that principle. Generally speaking, our children are learning that what is fun about sport are the experiences that we discover for ourselves or share with others.

There are many labels for all the generations of youth that have followed mine. There have been many studies to determine the characteristics of each generation. In my experience, the one characteristic that has impacted all of them and that has changed the world of sport is "consumerism." These kids (and some are now adults) are conscientious consumers. They do not feel compelled to buy anything that does not appear to provide some value. So, if you are "selling" sport or if you are "selling" your club or team, you better know your customer. I love these younger generations! They are so analytical in their approach to their choices: "So, if I come and play for you. what kind of benefits (wink, wink) will I receive?

"Well, you are eight years old. so, I'm thinking you might make some friends. Other kids might think you are cool. But mostly you will likely just have fun."

"*Sold!* "I'm in. when do practices start?"

Thank the universe for lovely children who just want to feel good and play! Therein lies our greatest opportunity as coaches. Teach them to play and let them feel good. Therein lies our greatest reward!

At the beginning of my coaching career, I was lucky enough to coach a provincial U19 women's team. It was a wonderful time when the sport of rugby was so new to this woman that selection simply involved allowing those who desired to play the opportunity. We were lucky if twenty-five young females wanted to play at this level, so the need to cut anyone was eliminated. That did not mean that the quality of our players was in any way diminished. In total contrast, we attracted the most dedicated, talented and courageous individuals that I have had the pleasure to coach.

I was employed with the Alberta Rugby Union at the time. We had placed a call for volunteer coaches for this new genre of rugby. No response. No coaches equal no program. One of the player's mothers contacted me to ask me when the tryouts were for this team, and wasn't it so exciting, and what a great sport this was, and how her daughter had found rugby to be this lifeline, and when were those tryouts again? I explained to her that we were experiencing some difficulty finding a coach, which placed the entire program in jeopardy. I can still hear her voice to this day as she paused slightly and said in a clear and trusting voice: "What about you? I hear that you are a pretty good coach?"

I sputtered somewhat and said: "Well, even if I could, or did. we don't have a manager, and there simply is no way that I have the time to do all that by myself."

"So, what does a manager do?" she asked innocently.

"Oh well, there is a great deal of work involved with that," I replied piously. "My goodness, you have to feed them, you have to find and get uniforms for them, you have to organize their training sessions, you have to organize their travel to games… Oh yes, it is an incredible amount of work," I emphatically stated.

"It sounds like being a mom," she laughed.

I remember the moment so clearly as I paused on the other end of the telephone line knowing exactly where we were headed. "Precisely," I said.

"Well," she giggled, "I can do that."

The rest is history. I met Kerry Yeo in person the following Saturday at the U19 Women's provincial camp. Kerry, her daughter Summer, and a collection of their friends and anyone else who was interested became the impetus for that first team. It was the first time I had experienced popsicles after practice and her trademark "snack packs." I have never wanted to coach without Kerry since that time.

We held a camp in Canmore, Alberta, right smack in the middle of the Rocky Mountains. We invited anyone who was remotely interested in helping our cause. Kerry came as the manager and I made my sister, Lolita, come to help her. Paul Howe came from Medicine Hat with his players; Cardi came from Calgary with her contingent; and Pat Forsythe came from Sherwood Park with her clan; and finally, as always, my long-suffering and dedicated friends, Ric Suggit and Maxi Miciak, came to help me coach. The mountains have always called to me and provided me with the peace to find clarity. So here we were training in my home place and creating this environment for these young women to explore themselves and find their way into this mosaic.

There was a young woman who attended, who was a solid, strong mobile prop. That would equate somewhat to a lineman if we were playing football. She was in her last year of eligibility in terms of age and had found rugby in her last year of high school. Melanie was not what the world would have endorsed as beautiful by magazine standards, but she was so beautiful to me. She had the most incredibly innocent and open eyes that shone with her positive spirit. She was so excited and enthusiastic to simply participate in any activity. She would throw her arm in the air to volunteer to hold the pop bags. She would throw her arm in the air to carry the water bottles. She was the first in line for sprints and the last to leave the field after kicking practice. She would seek to participate and contribute in any possible way. She was simply sucking up every second of this opportunity!

I was inspired by her undeniable positive spirit. She had this incredible appreciation for absolutely every opportunity to be part of anything that was being presented. Melanie had her nineteenth birthday while we were in Canmore and in true "mom" form Kerry had a cake, ice cream, candles, and a special group rendition of *Happy Birthday*. Melanie cried these great crocodile tears and exclaimed that she had never experienced such a wonderful birthday in her life. I want you to know that this young woman had wonderful parents who encouraged her and taught her to believe in herself and that according to them, she did not have any significant negative experiences in her life. She simply had never experienced complete and unconditional love and acceptance into a group of her own peers. Though she had been on teams previously, she had never felt part of the actual fiber of the tapestry. That feeling of belonging, of being valued, of being loved for who you are is a powerful emotion.

Melanie would later write in a thank you card: *Helen, I have played many sports and been coached by many coaches, and you truly change lives.*

This time it was my turn to cry big crocodile tears, because in fact Melanie changed my life. She was the total confirmation for me that there may not be an "I" in team, but there is a distinct requirement for "us" and "we"—just the way we are, in our simplest and most vulnerable form. From that point on, my goal in coaching was to provide a valuable learning experience for all our players regardless of the outcome.

Maxi Miciak and Helen coaching the Pandas

Chapter 8
Playing the Nanapoopoo Game

As children we all learn lessons in humility and create techniques that allow our egos to survive what are at times painful experiences. One such technique that was common in my part of the world was the use of the word "nanapoopoo." "Nanapoopoo" had many definitions. It was a word that was acceptable for children to use to express an adult statement akin to, "Screw you, I don't care what you say, I am right!"

It could also mean: "See? I am right and I hope you feel bad!"

In addition, it could provide an exit strategy to a humiliating situation, "This sucks! I feel humiliation and I don't have any appropriate response, so I'm leaving!"

It was an acceptable response for children who were learning to cope with the world around them relative to the expanding ego inside of them. As an adult there is a societal expectation that we have learned how to cope with the dichotomy of reconciling our inner emotions with the forces of a sometimes-harsh external reality. That evolutionary achievement might be stunted in some of us, but the expectation if us as adults able to cope is still there.

In the world of games and sport, we are subject to a great range of experiences and emotions. In many ways sporting games mirror the bigger game of life. The euphoria of victory is offset by the trauma of defeat. The players of these games are very often completely uninspired or even powerless to change either what is happening in the course of the game or the outcome. It is infinitely easier to deal with the euphoric highs than the painful and sometimes crippling lows. I would venture to say that one of the most valued skills in the art of coaching lies in the coach's ability to deal with the lows being experienced by their athletes. The ability to change the perspective of the players from negative to positive is truly a talent. These opportunities for the growth of the individual athlete are often overlooked or wasted because the coach can be so negatively impacted by their own disappointment, that they miss the opportunity to guide or assist anyone through this drama in a positive way.

Winning, though it can provide great joy, doesn't always provide the participants with opportunities for learning and growth. One's ego can accept all the accolades bestowed upon it, and graciously watch as the game plan is being executed to a positive outcome. It can seem analogous to surfing a wave right to the shore without falling off. The ride is relatively easy and the sense of fulfillment relatively satisfying. Society tends to accept any coaching philosophy and style that results in success. Generally, if the coach is successful, they have obtained the right to the behavior of their choice, whether that is gracious acceptance of the opposition's superior performance or the rude indifference of no acknowledgment at all. A win means the plan has worked. The team's performance is good enough to tick off a notch in the win column. The emotions related to winning tend to be positive—pride in the players' performance and pride in the coach's ability to help them succeed. The desired outcome has been achieved and all seems well with the world of the athletes and also with the coach. There is an old saying that reflects a common opinion of those who have experienced winning: "If it ain't broke, don't fix it."

However, in sport, as in life, it is in the "falling off" that most lessons are learned. In the emotionally charged moment of failure, most participants are resistant to the idea that this moment could also be a pivotal point of learning. Most of us do not acknowledge moments of failure or loss as learning opportunities for which we should be grateful. It is a common reaction to actually hate these moments because they hurt! They remind us of our vulnerabilities and life's inequities. These moments of failure provide an opportunity for self-evaluation, for review of information, for increased motivation and to ask the questions we don't ask ourselves when we win. The ensuing questions are difficult and about who we are, what we are doing, and perhaps more importantly—why. It is a cliché to say that losing is not what is important, but rather how we respond to losing that matters. There is a reason this statement is overused in sport. There is a great deal of baggage attached to losing—baggage that ultimately affects how we respond. The amount and type of baggage that we carry is directly related to how we respond to the additional baggage involved in failure.

Losing has long been given a bad reputation. There is an underlying fear that when we lose, we are susceptible to taking on the characteristics of "losers." The characteristics of losers have never been empirically defined but it is safe to conclude that they are negative and not desirable. There is also a theory that losing too often can make you a "terminal loser." The assumption is that 'losers' have somehow forgotten how to win.

Failure is simply part of a process of learning. It is neither negative or positive. It is part of a repetitive cycle of experimentation, observation of results, and the corresponding re-evaluation of plans made to create positive outcomes. Failure or loss is a non-issue in the world of science. Most scientific hypotheses do not achieve legitimacy until they have travelled a long and exhausting path of experimentation that includes failure and which ultimately leads to a conclusion. Losing or failing should be an opportunity for learning. Losing should provide motivation for a re-evaluation of the process and acute investigation of detail and approach. Failure or losing gives us impetus to change our ideas or plans, or to create new ones. Researchers are constantly failing until they learn enough information from those failures to verify a truth. Sport does not appear to have the same patience. Losing is losing is losing.

Losers in sport carry a stigma. This stigma can corrupt their personal self-esteem, and this is especially so when there is little else in the life of an athlete or coach. We lost the game and therefore we are losers. That is a powerful and negative translation. It should then come as no surprise that athletes and coaches need to protect themselves from the stigma of losing. At the very least, we coaches need to be able to deflect failure or loss to someone else—anyone else, except ourselves.

For athletes, the deflection is fairly easy. We had the wrong strategy, the wrong game plan, the wrong preparation—the wrong coach!

"Whoa—hold the phone a minute, this is the coach you are talking about." And the coach retorts," If you, the player, hadn't dropped the ball in the open field, or if you had made that tackle, or if you had performed better, the result would have been different."

This is the beginning of the 'nanapoopoo' game. It's the athlete's fault, or it's the coach's fault, or it's the referee's fault, or it's the weather's fault, and it has to be someone's fault. Because it *cannot* be my fault. Because *I don't want to be a loser!*

It is common to use blame as a tool for avoiding the responsibility of our own actions, particularly if we are not proud of certain actions. Positive actions do not require blame, they are identified and claimed by the participant willingly. It is when we don't want to claim our action or inaction that blame becomes a potential tactic. The 'blame game' finds its roots embedded in the negative experiences of loss and failure. The domino effect that results from the fear of loss and failure and its corresponding stigma can result in behaviors that take us back to a time when we were equally unequipped to respond appropriately. That's right! I said *nanapoopoo!*

When I coached women's rugby at club level, there were a limited number of teams in the Edmonton area. This meant that teams could play each other numerous times over the course of a season rather than the standard home and away schedule. This overexposure to each other resulted in fierce rivalries. The team that I was coaching at the time had experienced a particularly painful loss to an arch rival. The opposition had obtained the services of an outstanding national team player. This player possessed a natural inside step and was so talented that she could cut through our defense like it was butter. She proceeded to do just that without any empathy for her obviously inferior opposition. In fact, this player appeared to be enjoying her destruction of our back line, smiling at them on her jaunt back from the scoring try. I could feel the burning humiliation of the player who had clearly been tagged as the 'point of penetration.' The opposing team was relentless. Because of the confrontational history between the two teams, there would be no mercy. They rang in try after try (a try in rugby is the same as a touchdown in football), scoring almost at will. I was powerless to help my team and in particular my dear little athlete whom they had chosen as the weak link. Moving her to another position would only move their attack and heighten the humiliation. The damage had been done. We were losing with a capital 'L' and we couldn't stop the bleeding. All we could do was hope the referee might call the game early. I could so vividly feel my players' pain and suffering and all I could do was suffer along with them. When the loss is so public and so excruciating for the players, it can become difficult for the coach to immediately provide any kind of healing words that don't sound cliché. Sometimes it is better to say nothing at the time and take some time to process the event before re-evaluating. Everyone agreed after the game that we would simply head to the showers and lick our wounds, and talk later when our wounds weren't so raw. The only problem with that decision was that I, as coach, had no opportunity to vent or release any of the pain and tension that I was carrying.

Rugby has been called "a ruffian's game played by gentlemen" and there is a great deal of tradition that accompanies the game. One of the traditions is for the opposing teams to form two lines at the end of every game and shake hands with the opposition and thank the referee. Needless to say, at this point I was experiencing the ultimate "loser" type of fear and humiliation that I referred to earlier in this chapter. I suppose after all that I have said to this point about the impact of failure and loss on the game's participants, it is not surprising that I had a real "nanapoopoo" moment. As both teams were lined up and in the process of shaking hands, I withdrew my hand and didn't shake the outstanding player's outstretched hand. It was shocking to both teams as I am a founder, teacher and long-standing pillar in this women's rugby community. It would be akin to Gandhi slapping away the hand of a follower. Clearly, I am not Gandhi. Clearly, it was not my proudest moment. But the experience of losing both the game and my composure in that moment was a pivotal point for me in coaching. It made me ask myself hard questions about my behavior and why I was coaching.

How had I succumbed to responding to loss and failure in such an unacceptable manner? When had losing become so abhorrent that I would behave so destructively? How had I strayed so far from my original intention? When I first started coaching all I wanted to do was help athletes reach their potential and use the medium of sport as a tool to help them in their growth and development as human beings. How did I degenerate to this point of ego-driven behaviors?

I believe that as humans seeking answers to questions regarding our own behaviors, we sometimes have to "go down the rabbit hole," or more specifically, inside of ourselves. I travelled back down my coaching path to the point where I had inadvertently accepted the notion that the outcome was more important than the performance. I had experienced success and it had provided me with that elusive approval I had always been seeking. The respect that I had worked so long and so hard to obtain. At the time I was happy to receive it and I didn't even notice my ego attach itself to every outcome from that point on. To continue to feel that heady, euphoric sense of value, I let go of the principles that had actually led me to that success in the first place. Losing became increasingly more difficult to accept. In particular, it became important not to lose to specific teams because somehow that loss reflected on the quality of my coaching. At this point, it wasn't about the athletes or the game—mostly it was about me and my ego. When ego is running your life, you can be assured there will be fear and self-doubt. Fear is how ego holds on to the control panel of our lives. It starts by presenting every negative "what if" scenario that could possibly occur. It locks itself in when you start imagining and then manifesting the outcomes of all your fears. It is a vicious cycle because the more you worry about those "what ifs," like the possibility of losing, the more you attract them to yourself. The more you lose, the more your fears are confirmed and the more negative energy you put into the one thing that is now consuming your thoughts—losing.

There is a book written by John Steinbeck called *The Summer of our Discontent*. That particular summer turned out to be the summer of my discontent. If humility was the lesson in life's curriculum, then I was first in line to learn it the hard way.

When you grow up the descendent of post-war German parents, there are generally two phrases you never hear: "I love you" and "I am sorry." As an educated and enlightened child of the '60s and '70s, I had come to grips with the first phrase. I couldn't easily verbalize my deep devotion and love for people. The physical demonstration of that love through hugging was still a bit of a challenge, but with the help of my children and my overtly affectionate friends, I was making progress. The problem with the second phrase is that you actually have to have some authentic emotional remorse to support the phrase in order for it to be believed. In my world, "I am sorry" means: "I am completely wrong and I beg your forgiveness." I am German. This DNA contains a strand of chromosomes that prevents us from thinking we have ever been *entirely* wrong. Misinformed? Yes. Misunderstood? Absolutely. Misguided? Possibly. But completely, unjustifiably and utterly, incorrect and wrong? That DNA molecule that makes us work relentlessly to pursue perfection is a 'pride' molecule. It comes from the 'ego' family and it has the capacity to corrupt your entire hard drive.

Drowning in the humiliation of what I had done, I quickly deflected my bad behavior to being equivalent to the bad behavior of the opposing coach. "That's right! If he weren't so badly behaved, I wouldn't be either!"

"It's not my fault!"

"It's. It's his fault!"

The phrase that reflects jumping from the fat to the fire could not have more aptly described my descent into the 'nanapoopoo' world of abject humiliation. I spent most of that summer searching my soul for the strength to take responsibility for my very public, ego driven and totally unacceptable behavior. If apologizing had been a little practiced skill prior to that event, I was certainly an expert by the end of the summer.

There is clarity that occurs when truth is accepted. The truth is that I was wrong to behave like that to the player. Particularly because I was in a position of authority as a coach. I was wrong to try and deflect my behavior to a completely innocent person. I spent that summer apologizing to the player, to the coach, to other players, to the other coaches, to referees, to executive members, and any being that might have been in the vicinity on that day including the trees that surround the field. I can tell you this. I have learned to say, "I am sorry." I had a summer of practice and it is now an app on my internal hard drive.

This takes us to the beginning again. What if we didn't believe, losing was so bad? What if it was an opportunity for learning?

When I first started coaching, I was joyful in my delivery because even though I knew I didn't know very much, I knew how much I cared about the athlete's experience. It was my reason for being there and it gave me great satisfaction and joy, win or lose. It was fun! And that, I have come to realize, is the barometer. If there is no joy in your activity, if what you are doing does not ultimately make you feel good, you need to check who is at the control panel, you or your ego? Why are you doing this? Has it become something that has attached itself to your self-identification? If you are not a winning player, a winning coach, then who are you? Just a player? Just a coach? Is it enough to be just a player or just a coach? It was at one point. When we all started playing and coaching, that in itself was the source of our fund and joy. The American Rugby Union has done an extensive study trying to determine why people play rugby and the predominant answer for all ages and genders is that they want to be around other rugby players.

It is the same thing we wanted when we were children—just a team to belong to.

Chapter 9
Fear, The Big Inhibitor

There are two major types of fear in sports: The athletes fear which is primarily derived from the 'what if I'm not good enough' collection of fears; and the other fear suffered by coaches which is primarily derived from the 'what if I'm not good enough' collection of fears.

Our dilemma is that no matter how spiritual our approach may be to whatever game we are coaching and playing, our 'success' in society is measured by the ominous 'win/loss' column. Coaches may stand in front of players and emphatically declare that winning is not important and that we are more interested in performance. As we as coaches deny the value of winning, we preach passionately that our greatest motivation as coach is to see them improve as players and celebrate their development. We have espoused all those philosophies that first convinced us that sport was a good environment. We believe in their growth as athletes and as individuals who are members of a larger community.

From the moment that my ego started telling me that I might be a good coach, a meaningful coach, perhaps even a successful coach, I started having disturbing dreams. These dreams weren't nightmares in the horror movie sense of nightmares, but I came to learn that these were 'my coaching' nightmares. The nightmares were different variations on a repeating theme. In one, I dreamt that I was giving the pre-game speech and everyone kept talking and no one would listen to me. It was as if they couldn't hear me. I kept yelling louder and louder, but no one could hear, or perhaps more likely no one would listen. Another version of the same 'fear' dream was that I walked onto the rugby field and there was someone else coaching in my place. I didn't really want to admit this here, but as I am apparently confessing all my dreams I may as well expose *all* my insecurities. I had been replaced by a young, male coach with a foreign accent. No one had told me about being replaced and no one seemed to notice that I was both shocked and terribly hurt. All the players greeted me as usual and the practice just kept rolling along led by this new coach. I just stood there completely humiliated and defeated.

Clearly it does not take a very senior psychologist to interpret these sad vignettes. My point here is that even though I was the biggest advocate for attaching myself to the performance and not the outcome, my fears were anchored in a belief system that firmly measured success by winning and losing and not by how well we played. Somewhere deep down in my subconscious there was an imprint that said: "While it is noble to advocate a spiritual approach to coaching, let's be real—winning is the real measure!" It isn't about who I am, it is about what I have achieved and what others think of me. The same ego that humbly acknowledged previous success was letting me know that the value of my performance was based on the win/loss column. I was afraid that if I didn't continue to win and be successful no one, not players or anyone else, would see me as credible or valuable. At this point I had started to connect the way that I coached with a successful outcome. If I didn't continue to be successful, then the way that I coached would no longer be credible. It took me a while to identify these fears. Fear can be like seepage flooding your basement. You don't notice that the basement is flooded until you step into two inches of water when you down there. You coach, you preach, you develop, you motivate, you inspire, but you don't win. Never mind! Winning is not the goal, remember? Performance is the goal. The player's experience is the goal. You know what you think you believe and yet you can't shake that "yukky" feeling, that "what the hell?" feeling—that "am I doing the right thing?" feeling. At that point, you start doubting yourself. You start second-guessing your strategies. You start questioning your drills, the quality of training sessions, until you are right smack in the middle of your biggest "not good enough fear."

My biggest fear was that the players would not have confidence in my ability to guide them to their best performances. They would stop listening to me or believing what I told them. They would think that I was *not* a good coach. Now it occurs to me that everything that I had read to that point clearly pointed out the hazards of relying on sources outside of yourself for your confidence and self-love. But sometimes when you are in the frame you can't see the picture. The immediate response to this fear is to arm yourself with every current piece of information you can lay your hands on. You become almost manic in your search for the "secret to success." Perhaps you need more schooling. Perhaps you need to immerse yourself in all the latest and greatest techniques. Perhaps you need to bloody well be on top of the most current information. Perhaps you need to be in the "right" programs with the "right" people. You no longer trust your instincts, so you start bringing in every "flavor of the month" technique you can find. If it's good enough for the most dominant national team in the world of rugby, the New Zealand All Blacks, it is good enough for you little buggers! Oh wait, you can't catch and pass. *Right*, OK, back to the drawing board. All your Gretzky strategies, solid common sense, and intuition are out the window along with your confidence. The situation is almost desperate. You start looking for clinics—anything to improve your performance as a coach. Now your ego drives your greatest "not good enough" fears.

I recall applying for a position as the national women's team coach. I would not have applied at that point in my career except for the fact that the job description of the position was so perfectly suited to my skill set. It was about creating a program across the country involving the development of U23s and the coordination of provincial programs in support of the national team program. I had already been the director of the national women's teams that had created the U23 program! Hello! That's my game! Creating co-operation and inclusion across the country. Building a program that supports the development of players and coaches. A top to bottom, holistic approach to moving athletes to their greatest potential! At this point, you need to stop the video. I was so excited about the prospect of creating a comprehensive program based on those original principles of performance that I didn't even see it coming!

A man with a Welsh accent called me and told me that the reason I was not getting the position was because I couldn't coach the "new game of rugby." I thought he was joking and I laughed. "Well, that's pretty handy, since most women in this country haven't mastered the old game yet." No laughter. Awkward pause. Hello ego. Let's take a little trip to the "beat me up" room. Clearly, I should have attended more clinics.

Coaches attend clinics not just to gain knowledge, but also to edify that what they are doing is correct according to coaches who are successful or trainers who at least profess to have the secret to success. The irony is that looking for the confirmation that you are a good coach from outside sources is transient at best. Confidence, for athletes or coaches, stems from an internal source. It comes from inside us, when we trust and believe in the values that guide our actions and choices. It is difficult at times to align our intentions with those values when the blueprint or self-belief in our subconscious are not congruent. Staying true to the ideal of service to athletes rather than being a slave to outcomes is difficult when you are a packing around a secret self-belief that winning is the measure of success and you may not be good enough. That self-belief is the spawning ground for all the fears that gurgle up to the surface when your athlete or team's performance is in the wrong 50th percentile. In many cases we aren't even aware that we have this self-belief. If you had asked me at the time whether I was fearful about being good enough, I would have emphatically denied it. I would have launched a long dissertation on my passion for coaching and my dedication to the dream of using sport as a medium for the creation of good human beings. This self-belief or blueprint that hangs out in our subconscious is usually a collection of all the experiences and judgments that we have absorbed over the course of our lives. If, in fact, we find out that we have negative or limiting self-beliefs, we need to make a conscious effort to change them to allow ourselves to escape the condemnation of our ego. Failure to let ourselves feel the hurt and pain and to acknowledge it, prevents us from ever letting it go.

When I was very young, I believed that I could run so fast, that I could fly. When I became a teenager complete with all the hormonal physiology that accompanies that age, I was told that I was strong but not fast. I have carried that belief with me for all my life, and consequently made choices that reflected my limitation regarding speed. I have never questioned or challenged that belief. I never realized that I believed that about myself.

Athletes are subject to the condemnation from their egos, as well. One of the best examples of the limits created by fear can be seen during try-outs or selection events where athletes are being pitted against each other in competition for a position on the same team. This situation is one of the best illustrators of how an athlete's "blueprint" can be limiting. Most athletes have been invited to these camps or tryouts because a scout or a coach has been impressed with their performance. Athletes whose blueprints reflect "I am unstoppable" and "I am fearless," step into situations with other athletes of comparable ability, but of an opposite blueprint— "I am not good enough" —and show superior performances. In many cases, these superior performances are not a result of superior skill or talents, they are the direct result of a self-belief. The challenge of coaching and bringing out the best in an athlete involves being able to put on your X-ray glasses and look deep into their beings and see this negative blueprint. The art of coaching involves work with the athlete to make them aware of their self-belief and of the collective effort to change it.

In 2005, I was coaching the national U23 women's program. We created a program that was entirely developmental in nature. This program was designed to teach these athletes how to become senior national team members. The goal of the program was to teach them the skill sets required to reach their potential, hopefully resulting in their selection to the national team. The program was created to gather these athletes from across the country and spend the summer developing their skills and measuring their skills against various levels of competition but capping the summer off with two back-to-back games against the United States U23s.

Thirty players, two full teams of young women who had no idea of what was going to happen or what they should expect to happen, landed on the Edmonton tarmac. My friend Kerry had addressed the most important issues concerning athletes; food and sleep. Again, the University of Alberta proved to be our supporting ally and the girls were housed at St. Joe's residence, which allowed them to sleep two to a room and eat in a cozy cafeteria that doubled as our meeting room. I am a believer in energy. Good energy begets good energy. My friend Kerry has the most astounding level of positive energy and consequently everyone she works with provides her with everything she needs and substantially more. The girls had as much food as they wanted and most importantly, they had access to "grazing" food. They had access to the fitness and aquatic facilities for training and hydrotherapy. They had their own therapist, another friend and previous Panda, Kerry Crozier. This camp was possibly the most logistically sound and effective environment we had ever been able to create.

The first item on the docket was to provide the information the players required to become aware of their own thoughts and blueprints. My friend Maxi (previous Panda coach and national team player) hauled in 30 coil-bound journals and 30 pens and began to work with the players to recording their physical, emotional, and spiritual states. She advised them that we would not be reading these journals. These journals were the tools they required to identify what they were thinking, how they were feeling, and how they were performing. They were travelling notes for themselves to see if they could identify any blueprints that might be affecting their performance. They were ranting notes. They were technical notes. Most importantly, they were notes to themselves.

The first blueprint that we wanted to address was a perennial fear that most athletes possess, "I am not fit enough" and "I can't get fit enough." Again, thanks to Kerry's amazing ability to get the world for no cost, we were able to transport all the girls to the mountains and spend five days at a hostel. It was here, where nature can speak to you when no one else can, that many of these athletes dealt with this self-belief. I had involved my son Sean and my personal trainer, Duey Hume, to create a fitness experience for the girls that would require them to seek out their inner strength. Sean and Duey were incredibly creative in using the nature around them and providing a program that was balanced with laughter and tears of sheer exhaustion. The girls were challenged to listen only to their intuition and not to their ego. They were challenged to "show" themselves that they were in fact physically capable of much more than they believed. At this point, we had not even spoken of rugby positions or technique. Their goal was to survive this fitness ordeal. Their goal was to collectively conquer the mountain. It could only be achieved if each one of them was able to run to the top. It was pointless if anyone was left behind. Together, they pulled, prodded and carried each other to the top of the mountain. We used the opportunity to show them the power of community in this endeavor. This group of 30 girls was a team in the most authentic sense of the word before any of them even touched the rugby ball that summer. Many created tight bonds and have remained close friends since that time. Most importantly, when they came down off that mountain, they had all, if not replaced their existing blueprint, strengthened it to the point of "fearless." They had all run head first into their own 'walls' and come out the other side keenly aware that they possessed another level of potential. They had proven to themselves that they were much more than what their limiting blueprints had predicted.

In my other world, where mortgages must be paid and food has to be provided, I worked in providing disaster recovery programs for flood victims. That summer it rained, and it flooded in southern Alberta and I had to leave the program. I called my friend Neil Langevin from Lethbridge and asked if he could help me out with the program. Neil is a teacher and was able to come to Edmonton. He and Sean guided the girls through their rugby technical development. Rugby skills and technique are not so complicated that many coaches would differ to a great degree on their delivery. However, the idea that I had promised the girls that they would all *start* in the final games against the Americans floored both Sean and Neil. My intention was to eliminate the greatest fear of most athletes, the fear that they will not be selected to participate at all. Not being allowed to perform when one's prime purpose in life is to do just that—perform—is soul destroying. My intention was to take away the first, most primal of all fears— "not good enough" —and allow the chance to perform. You are here. You have already been chosen. You will play. I was emphatic that even though I could not be there, my promise would hold. Neil looked at me incredulously. "Don't you want to win?" he asked me. "Not as much as I want them all to feel like winners," I answered. Neil and Sean held true to my promise. Every one of those players started in one of the international games. How long they stayed on the field was up to them and their ability to perform under those conditions. Both teams performed brilliantly, and they won both games.

It is very difficult to hold to a philosophy and promote a way of thinking that is not supported by society. They don't put celebrated coaches in halls of fame for "developing" players. They don't usually recognize coaches who have impacted young lives in a meaningful way but haven't won anything. Nor do they place a great deal of value in a coach that provides a meaningful recreational experience for non-serious athletes. They recognize coaches who are successful, who win. Who win a lot. If a player is telling their friends that they play on a really great team, but they don't win very much, they are likely to elicit a snort and cocked eyebrow. Most players see themselves as contenders and they want to be challenged, so promoting the experience as simply fun may not attract the caliber of player that indeed makes it fun to coach. So there exists this dichotomy; on the one hand, the coach wants to provide this meaningful experience to athletes and place the emphasis on the performance not the outcome; but on the other hand, the coach needs the success of wins to keep the "not good enough" fears at bay. Here is my advice: Punt the "not good enough fears" and listen to your intuition!

If believing in yourself and your abilities and philosophies is a challenge for an athlete, it could well be a coach's greatest challenge. Trying to discern the voice of ego from the voice of your intuition can be a confusing process. Many times, when I thought I was hearing my intuition, I was actually hearing my ego. It was only at the point where I would ask myself, "Why are you doing this Helen?" that I would realize it was for the total appeasement of my ego. I had convinced the players that their performance and not the outcome was important, but I kept getting sucked into the vortex of success. It feels good, it gives you that addicting attention, it validates your process and ultimately, it validates you. Hold the phone! That's where we started this chapter. I am the only one who can truly validate me. I am the only person I must answer to. I am the one who knows when I am authentic and when what

I am doing is providing me the joy I am seeking. It is when I get rid of all that self-judgment and I start to appreciate and love who I am and what I am doing, that I can hear my intuition again.

When we coach from an authentic love of what we are doing and who we are trying to teach, we simply can't go wrong. If walking onto the field, court, ice or any other surface makes you smile with an intrinsic joy you can't explain, you are in the right place. If seeing athletes and players smile with joy at their own performance gives you an exhilarating sense of purpose, you are doing the right thing. If supporting and guiding them through the challenges of their performances makes you cry too, you are doing the right thing. You always were and will continue to be good enough!

Chapter 10
Barefoot Flying

One of my later coaching experiences played out like one of those movies where you are expecting the antagonist to overcome all obstacles and achieve their long-sought-after victory. You know the story is almost over and you want to see the hero triumphantly pumping the air in victory as the credits roll. You are watching and waiting and then in some twist of the story line, the hero doesn't pump fists in the air, but rather learns some profound lesson and smiles quietly, walking away from the contest entirely and exits into the sunset. What? What? What the hell? I'm pissed now! Stupid movie! Don't they know what we want? We want happy successful endings! Well, at least happy endings where the hero gives up winning for the greater good. Not where they don't even play! How anticlimactic is that?

This coaching venture was a lesson in authenticity. The Druids Rugby Football Club has a women's program with junior players and two senior teams. The simple fact that three female teams exist on one club is a credit to the quality of the leadership in that club. They were already successful before I came into the picture. Successful, in my opinion, because they had in the past, and still were, attracting young women to play rugby. Clearly, these individuals were enjoying their experience. Many of the senior girls that were playing first division rugby had played for the University of Alberta Pandas while I had been coaching those teams. When they asked me if I would consider coaching them, I think deep down subconsciously, they were hoping that I could replicate those previous "successes." I think that I too was still holding on to a blueprint that was measuring my value based on previous successes. If I were being completely honest, I think I was also hoping I could reproduce those previous "successes." That would be validation that my "spiritual" approach to coaching was in fact "successful." How ironic. Here I am proposing that sport needs to change its addiction to wins and losses and its current measure of "success." How am I supporting my argument? I am using the same measurement tools—wins and losses. I think I mentioned this in previous chapters. Sometimes, when you are in the frame, you can't see the picture. As I grow older, I also realize that having learned a lesson once does not mean the same challenge will not appear again.

Panda pre-game focus

In addition to subconsciously wanting to prove my theories, I sincerely loved coaching. And I loved coaching with my son, Sean[4]. In typical first-generation Canadian fashion, I have never told him how much I admire his

---

[4] One of the many blessings of my coaching experience has been the opportunity to coach with my children. Both Amanda and Sean were the unsolicited benefactors of many coaching sessions and clinics. I hauled those two kids everywhere I went. At the age of 13, Amanda was the youngest Level One coaching participant. I needed her to fulfill the criteria of at least eight participants in a clinic that I was delivering in Saskatoon, Saskatchewan. Poor pumpkin, after traveling 12 hours in our sturdy grey mini-van, she had to act as my tackling dummy. Amanda was a sweetheart, complying with all my requests, but the passion of competitive sport was not in her blood. Sean on the other hand had already drunk the cool aid through his first sporting passion of hockey. He had a natural kinship to the art of coaching.

coaching skills and abilities. Unlike myself, my son has always played sports with the true spirit of an "artist." The ice and the field have always been his canvas and his ability to create offence through skillful playing has been his paint brush. He is an authentic performer. His joy in performing and participating is real. He truly loves playing. He is at home on the ice or on the field. Sean is a fierce competitor and some of his antics in junior hockey would belie that sweet innocent grin of his. Most importantly, when it comes to sport, Sean's blueprint carries no fear. He coaches with the same joy and confidence he plays with. He loves winning, but it isn't because it is a measure of how successful he is, it's because more than anything else in the world, he wants his players to feel the joy of excellence in performance that he felt as a player. The only time that Sean gets into trouble when he is coaching is when he feels his player's pain. Though he is relatively young in years, he succumbs to what I call the "papa bear syndrome." This syndrome is again based on the negative impact that losing brings to sport. In the same way that we hated the humiliating feeling of being a loser when we played, we almost can't bear to see that inflicted on our players. In response to protecting them from this pain, we become "bears protecting our cubs at all costs." I love the passion in Sean. I love the ease with which he creates practice sessions that challenge, teach, and excite the players. I believe, and he may not, that someday he may find that his true purpose in life will be coaching. He is authentic. He is a natural. Coaching with him has been one of my joys in life.

When Sean and I began coaching the Druids, I made it clear to them that I was not interested in outcomes, only performance. I indicated that probability supports the idea that when performance levels were excellent, there was an equal probability that the outcomes could reflect that positive performance. Why did I add that second part? I think I added it because firstly, I believe it to be true, but also because I was concerned that they would not buy into this "spiritually" based coaching philosophy on its own merit. I needed to convince them using the tried-and-true measure of "success." Again. How ironic? Here I am preaching excellence in performance as the true measure of our success and then in the same breath, I am using the old win/loss success scenario to validate that belief. My fears were already peeking through the bushes.

The first season of coaching the Druids was one of the most enjoyable seasons of coaching that I had ever experienced. I was coaching with my son, and many times spitting out instructions with my newborn grandson Wyatt in my arms. One of my most treasured memories is coaching how to scrummage with Wyatt sleeping in my arms, and one of the players happily moving in to hold him, while I moved into the front row to demonstrate a technique. The girls who played for the Druids were a delightful collection of truly "happy" girls. Both Sean and I were challenged to come up with pregame talks that would create the sense of intensity required for focused and serious performance. Many seriously intentioned sessions ended up in fits of giggling laughter. Both teams responded positively to the type and quality of coaching they were receiving. The increased individual skill level for all players provided them with the ammunition they needed to defeat teams who had previously defeated them. The girls began to appreciate their own camaraderie and the value of their community. There was no first team or second team; there were only players available for Wednesday or Saturday games. At the end of the first year, the girls played in both final games of the two women's divisions, winning the regional second division. Their performances were significantly enhanced, and success stepped out of the bushes.

In the following year, as the performance levels continued to rise, so did the expectations. Success was not only out the bushes; he was beckoning under the goal posts. They were playing such good rugby that on many occasions, they themselves were surprised by the quality of their performance. There were games when I could only grin and gush with pure happiness about how well they had played. There were, in contrast, games that exposed our weaknesses related to fitness and the fact that we had many new and inexperienced players. As both teams continued to progress, and players were selected for representative teams, the expectations continued to rise. At the peak of my time with this club, we had all three teams in the provincial finals. I must reiterate that to have three women's teams is a momentous success. To have three teams in provincial finals is worthy of pride for the entire organization. The junior coach took his team to a successful conclusion winning the provincial title. Sean took the first team to Calgary and was defeated by a Calgary team, who for all intents and purposes, was the regional representative team complete with four or five national players. I do not say that to insinuate any "sour grapes" or unfair tactics. I say that to give an indication of how well this club team performed regardless of the outcome.

On my final day of coaching the Druids, this collection of young players, the Wednesday team (or the second team), far surpassed any expectation I had for their performance. They were the lightest, smallest pack (front line players) on the face of the earth. From somewhere inside themselves, they pulled the will and the ability to push a pack twice their size off the ball. By half-time, they were at least 15 points behind the opposition. By the end of the game, they were down by three points and trying to position themselves for a drop kick. "A drop kick?" A drop kick is where a player obtains possession of the ball in the heat of the action and has both the skill and the presence of mind to drop the ball onto the ground and then kick it precisely through the goal posts. In professional rugby, that skill is only performed by the most confident and skilled players in the game. It is one of the most challenging skills in the game of rugby. It is also one of the most tactically effective ways to score points. Here they were, this group of giggly girls on the Wednesday team looking to use the same tactic that Johnny Wilkinson used to win the World Cup for England. Their performance was stellar, but the outcome was a loss. Following the game, the girls gathered on the deck. I was sipping on my beer within ear shot and I could hear them talking and laughing in that trademark Druid "happy girl" way. They were making plans for the evening and for the next year. They were disappointed to lose, but more importantly they were happy to play as well as they had. Were they quitting? Absolutely not! Were they excited to try again? Totally! Did they believe they could conquer the world? Without a doubt!

There seems to be a "condition," a "zone," a state of being that occurs when athletes describe their most outstanding performances. According to many of the stories retold, movement becomes effortless, the surrounding activity becomes inconsequential, time slows down, the athlete experiences a form of expanded vision and a natural execution of an intuitive activity. It feels like the perfect execution of inspiration. When teammates try to explain the feeling of a collective version of that condition, they call it a "perfect play." They often reflect that they were propelled by an intuitive force to expedite the movement in that particular manner at that particular time without any thought process.

When I was a small child, there was a meadow just below our farm house where the calves nibbled the sweet green clover to an inch of the ground. When it rained, the clover would be engorged with water and became a soft emerald carpet. I would race across the field in my bare feet and the wet clover would squeeze up between my toes. I would rise up on the balls of my feet and then higher right to the end of my toes. I would accelerate to the point where I felt I could fly. I was weightless, powered by the sheer joy of the movement and unencumbered with any knowledge of limitations. Then I lifted, and soon, I was… "barefoot flying."

I have dedicated my life to returning to that moment of authentic joy as often as I can. There have been occasions as a coach, where I have witnessed athletes who have performed at a level far beyond anything I had seen them do prior to that point. It is as if there is a collective consciousness that unites their spirit to perform these activities almost effortlessly. They intuitively seem to know where to be in support, when to change their pace, what angle to run at—and all of this at top speed. I believe that they are allowing themselves to experience the sheer joy of playing. At the risk of landing in the "cuckoo" category, I believe that the joy of playing is what we are truly seeking when we embark in a sport. We want to go barefoot flying, without any restrictions or inhibitions or fears holding us to the ground. Some of us even want to share that feeling with others and watch "miracles" happen.

As coaches, I believe the greatest gift we can provide to our athletes is to care about them enough to allow them to be who they are and give them the opportunity to experience the joy of playing. That same joy that we experienced as innocent children, before we started trying to be good at anything.

We can accept them for who they are without judgment. We can provide them with the empathy they need to keep trying. We can teach them to be courageous by being vulnerable. We can love them. Now when I say "love your players," I don't mean "*love*" your players. We can arm them with the skills they require to fully participate in the contest. We can teach them how to make decisions. We can prepare them with the strategy that we think might best assist their efforts. Then we can put them on the stage, turn on the lights, and let them play! When they glance at you with that flushed look that says, "Oh my god, did you just see what I did? This is so fun!" You can sigh a deep satisfied sigh and know that you have provided the opportunity for one more person to go barefoot flying. How much fun is that?

Chapter 11
Hope and Humor
What We All Need

In my life I have played three roles that have been the primary source of my personal growth and development: Player, coach and mother. Though I must say that every once in a while, being a partner in a relationship can send a lesson or two as well. Throughout the millions of events that continue to remind me who I really am and what the hell I am doing here, there have been two themes that have played a predominant role in my survival. Regardless of where I am or what I am doing, there needs to be a ray of hope, some small light beam that I can leap for and clutch and hold on to for dear life. In addition, I need to feel the gurgle of a giggle bubbling up from somewhere inside me as I hang helplessly dangling from a ray of hope.

As a young farm girl, growing up in the interior of British Columbia, I was never allowed to participate in sports at school. It was a frivolous activity that would prevent me from completing the many tasks waiting for me at home. To participate, I would have to answer positively to a mega list of chores requiring completion. I remember thinking, *All I have to do is make sure that all the work is done before asking permission to go.* My little "Hitler-mom" never said I couldn't go, she said I had to complete the mega list before I could go. Hope. I would rope my dad into helping me check off the list. I don't think he ever really understood why I wanted so desperately to participate, but he was impressed with my tenacity. Most of all I think he also wanted me to have hope. He was the epitome of hope. An immigrant dirt farmer mired in clay and poverty with "Pa Cartwright" dreams of creating his own Ponderosa. He taught me how to dream. He taught me to find that beam of light and hang on for all I was worth.

Hope is the essence of humanity. It is the gas that moves the engine. Without hope, we likely wouldn't try anything. It is an unyielding belief that what we seek is possible. It is that intuitive connection to our soul that prompts us to reach for something that seems unattainable but somehow divinely motivated. In Canada, there are ice rinks full of young hockey players with little hearts pumping hope to their dreams of playing in the Olympics or the National Hockey League. In New Zealand, there are fields full of young rugby players with little hearts pumping hope to their dreams of being on their national teams: The All Blacks or the Black Ferns. Throughout the world and throughout time, hope has allowed this human species not to just survive but to blossom into the flowers of our imagination.

When I was a player, all I needed was a sniff of hope to keep me trying, to keep me engaged, involved, and most importantly dreaming. Sport provides an environment that fosters hope. The idea that anything is possible is the food that feeds our love affair with "underdogs." So many of us have experienced the harsh reality of the world where hopes and dreams are diminished to a point where trying is discarded as a preordained wasted effort. Sport, on the other hand, provides this delicious history that tells tales of the unexpected, the unexplainable, the unpredictable, and ultimately the impossible. The feats exist and are clearly recorded in the history books. Most importantly they stand as towering beacons of hope for all of us. That is why we play; because we hope. We hope we will be chosen. We hope we will play well. We hope we will fulfill our destiny. We hope we will play again and again and again. until we don't want to anymore or just can't.

Helen, Kerry, and Amanda (player) in the Grey Cup parade in Edmonton

When I was a young child growing up in the shadows of World War II and immigrant poverty, my family created a coping mechanism that has served me well over time.

When things were so bad that the only thing you could do was cry. Someone would crack some sarcastic remark and we would giggle. Sometimes we giggled at the inappropriateness of the comment, the bad timing, and the shocked face response it would elicit. Sometimes it would be a simple physical function that couldn't be contained. God bless farts and burps, especially from those who maintain the standard of control most of the time. It would inevitably lead to a pause in the drama, a moment of awkward silence and then a bubble of laughter would escape from someone, generally infecting everyone else. Soon the moment of crisis had been defused to one more of life's ironies or one more challenge from an unrelenting list of obstacles.

I am reminded of a time when a new team that we were creating—the Coven—were playing against the Rockers in one of our first encounters. At that time, it was hard to convince referees to facilitate our games. There was a resistance to the idea of women playing this type of combative sport. We didn't attract the most qualified or experienced officials. The Rockers were renowned for the size, strength and expertise of their "pack." As I have mentioned before, the pack is akin to football's front linemen. The coven front line was composed of Franny on my left, myself in the middle at hook and June on my right. At this point, I was still playing the game and not coaching yet. We had two absolutely novice second rows behind us, whose slender basketball body types didn't add a lot to our total mass. In rugby, as in most games, possession of the ball is a mandatory requirement of offence. The Rockers were big, and they were strong, and they knew how to scrummage. We, on the other hand, were not so big, not so strong, and not so experienced. We knew that if we could just get the ball to Corrine, our talented Scrum half, and out into the open field, we could have a chance at scoring. The Rockers knew that too and proceeded to play to their strengths. They pushed us off every ball. For those of you not familiar with rugby that means losing all your face offs or losing all your jump balls. No ball means no scoring points. It became clear that we needed some "out of the box" thinking. I secretly suggested to Franny, June, and our two gangly second rows that every time the ball moved into the Rockers possession that we would "accidentally" fall down. In the game of rugby, there are situations that can be dangerous. A collapsing scrum, or a scrum that "falls down" is certainly one of them. Risk management of the game dictates that everyone practices a protocol for how that can happen without anyone getting hurt. No one in rugby ever collapses a scrum intentionally. Well, almost no one. My suggestion was that we would take advantage of our referee's inexperience and gently take the scrummage to ground, but scream in agony at the same time, so that he would absolutely believe that this was happening "accidentally." The first time it happened, it was perfect execution. Gentle decline of the front row to ground and the appropriate amount of feigned injury. The result was as expected, reformation of the scrum. Do it again? Success. Most plans don't work right off the bat. This was no exception. It took us three "gently" collapsed scrums before we got possession of the ball. In the meantime, the Rockers front row had realized what was happening and kept yelling at the referee that we were cheating. He was a good man with a good heart and could not conceive that the innocent faces he was looking at would ever consider such a treachery. In hindsight, the plan was reckless, but it was successful. We got the ball out of the scrummage and into the hands of players with stealth and speed and the ability to score. Score they did! And as predicted, we won the game 4-0.

The piece of this story that has been omitted is the piece where we had not informed our coach of our despicable plan. He had no idea what we were doing, or that we were doing it intentionally. To our young English postdoc coach, it appeared to have been the worst display of rugby that he had ever seen, and he told us that as soon as we reached the sidelines. Let me correct that statement. He didn't "tell" us that, he "screamed" it at us. And there it was. That awkward silent moment. dangling like ripe fruit in front of my face. "Whew, I can't imagine what you would have said if we had lost." It starts with a twitch of a smile, invades shoulders that begin to shudder, moves into stuttered giggles, and finally erupts into a full-blown, uncontainable belly laugh. I loved my teammates. They allowed themselves to be moved from the drama of the moment to a releasing belly laugh. The young English postdoc coach. Not so much.

There are situations in sport, where a coach or an official is trying to create a memorable moment of drama and intensity. These moments are designed to penetrate the player's psyche and change a thought process or ignite their motivation.

In 2006, under the driving force of Roger Smith, the then Rugby Canada president, I was on the organizing committee of the Women's Rugby World Cup, held in

Edmonton, Alberta, Canada. This was the first time that the Canadian public would be able to see this quality of female rugby up close. The final games were being played at Commonwealth Stadium and the tournament involved 12 teams from around the world who had winning performances at the previous World Cup in Spain. This was truly the "big time" for those of us who had created, developed and promoted this game for women in Canada and the rest of the world.

Helen and Anna Schnell at Anna's selection to the National team

Pandas Championship

The Canadian National team was being coached by my friend Neil Langevin. Neil had invited me to participate in a tradition that the women's team had initiated in previous years. It was the presentation of the team jerseys to the players prior to the final games. I was so honored! I was so excited! I wanted it to be so special and inspiring! I wrote a speech based on our Canadian heritage of being "tough" and how that "toughness" is created by facing and eliminating your fears. I suggested in my speech that the only thing that can hold you back from achieving all your dreams is fear. It was my intention to create a dramatic gesture that would symbolize an elimination of those fears. Under the spell of drama and excitement, I had a large stamp created that read: *Fuck You Fear*. It was eight inches high and about 16 inches wide. I asked my friend Kerry to find some red ink that we could use to create this emphatic declaration.

Everyone filed into the meeting room. All the players, all the staff, all the families. Oh. oh. I didn't realize families were invited. *Hmmmmm, this might be a bit awkward?*

Oh well, too late to turn back now, carry on! After my speech, I invited all the players to pick up the pens and the paper that Kerry had so diligently spread on the tables. They were invited to write down the fears that might have arisen through this competition. They were to bring their written fears to the front of the room, crumple up the paper, throw it into the garbage, take the stamp, stamp the large piece of paper hung at the front of the room, and collect their jersey. All this great dramatic gesture was to symbolize the elimination of any fears that might impede their dreams of success the next day.

The hotel meeting room was packed with players, officials, families and, of course, my collection of support staff. It was a basement room. Relatively generic in color but somewhat dimly lit, except where the large poster board paper hung. There was a nervous tension in the room that generally accompanies those preparing for a climatic performance. My speech had fulfilled its purpose and the room buzzed with electricity. Kerry, who oversaw making sure there was ink on the stamp, was so excited and somewhat distracted that she just kept squirting this bright blood red ink onto the stamp. The first player to participate in the ritual was the team captain. It is the captain's role to set the pace of the game. She defiantly ripped up her written recognition of her fears and threw them into the garbage. She grabbed the dripping stamp from Kerry's hands and hit the poster board with the velocity of boxer's round house punch. The room gasped! There, at the front of the room, was a highlighted white poster board, splattered in blood red ink with the words *fuck you fear* dripping ominous streams of red, blood red, ink onto the floor.

And there it was. that awkward silent moment.

It starts with a twitch of a smile, invades shoulders that begin to shudder, moves into stuttered giggles, and finally erupts into a full-blown, uncontainable belly laugh.

Hope and humor! According to Garth Brooks, life is not tried if it's merely survived, if you're standing outside the fire!

Chapter 12
The Closing

I have been writing this book for the past 10 years. Each time that I sit down to transfer my thoughts into meaningful deliberation and colorful stories, I remember yet another experience or story. I wondered at what point I would reach the end and how would I conclude[5] this ongoing screenplay of my life without dying first? It occurred at the beginning of 2018.

In 2017, my son approached me to do the "right thing." When a conversation starts with the justification and ends with the proposition it gives insight into the confidence of the "seller's" commitment to making a sale. Sean knew that I would likely resist his suggestion unless I could be sold on the idea. Most marketing strategies bounce the brilliant idea or proposal right out front and then support it with a plethora of sound reasoning. Needless to say, the idea of being president of a rugby club was not high on my bucket list and required a more compelling sales strategy. This particular

---

[5] I had started this love affair in 1977. Forty years later, it occurred to me that I finally had nothing left to say, or at least nothing that anyone was prepared to hear.

rugby club was not really "my" rugby club, it was more Sean, my son's, rugby club, the Clansmen Rugby Football Club in Edmonton, Alberta[6]. Though I had coached the seconds' team under the watchful eye of my friend, Ric Suggitt and I created relationships with those players, I had not been invited into the fold. I was an oddity, not just a black sheep, they had plenty of those, but more like a stray goat. A stray goat that would figure out soon enough that even though I was able to hang out with the herd, I wasn't actually a sheep and all the sheep knew it. Some of them didn't care and some of them actually liked it, but all of them knew it. Yeah. Goat, not sheep. Just to be clear.

So, the idea of taking the reins of leadership with this group gave me great pause for reflection. This wasn't my club, where I had a history, where there was a natural group of friends that I could call on for support. I didn't have my close circle of support that shared a vision and just needed my neurotic passion to drive it forward. No, this would be different. I only had a couple of old friends on this club, "bear" Ron Allen and Davie Graham. The players I had coached had long since retired. And that was Sean's most compelling argument. This was going to be the year of the Clan's 50th anniversary and there were a couple of missing generations. There hadn't been the traditional changing of the guard as in the years of past. The guard was completely missing! He was worried that the 50th anniversary would be embarrassing for Bear and Davie. These two icons of Clan rugby had been mentors for Sean and he cared deeply about

---

[6] Bear, (Ron Allen), Davie Graham and Dana Lowry are the patriarchs of the Clansmen Rugby Football Club.

them personally and about their most prized collection of grass, goal posts, and memories.

"Mom, there is no one there to make sure that the event comes off with the organization that it requires and that the rugby part of that event is not a humiliation of the current Clan players!"

Well, how can a friend abandon her friends? OK, I'm in.

For the record, the fiftieth celebration weekend was actually in the very capable hands of Kirby White, who over the years, has become the working hands of Ron Allen's dreams[7]. So, Kirby assembled his committee of lost guard and Dave Logan, Stephen Saunders (in conjunction with all the current rugby boys and girls) created a rugby play list for the day that saw the many graduating rugby classes playing the current contenders and all was well. I was at the helm, doing what has become my "thing," connecting the dots, soothing the egos, making sure that the details are covered. It's all in the details!

So here I was, 30 years later, at the same spot where I originally started. Club rugby. I had come full circle. It was the same game, but it was a different environment. It took a while for me to learn how to work with the new generation of young club executives, the millennials. They were aghast at the idea that I did not have the intricate knowledge of "cloud workings." They were shocked when I insisted that we assemble a master email list. They were angry when I suggested that the website not simply be a "landing site,"

---

[7] Kirby White, a former player.
Dave Logan and Steve Saunders are the club's current executive

but also be an "information site." At the first executive meeting that I attended, I was the source of contagious glee as they commented to each other via their phones on the various vintage ideas that were being presented by yours truly. When they realized that I had no idea what they were doing, it created such delight that they could not contain themselves and burst into uncontrollable laughter at my expense. At that point all the maternal instincts rose to the fore and I reverted to the same tactics that had served me so well through child rearing. I leaned over to the closest smirking little shit and whacked him on the head and made them all put their phones away.

Because I was no longer current on the delivery processes for club rugby, it took me some time to realize that though many things had changed, some very crucial things had not. The bulk of the responsibility for the delivery of grassroots rugby was still in the domain of the clubs, and they were the ones doing the heavy lifting in terms of getting this game out into the community. The interesting issue that arose for me was that the fees paid by every player under the age of 21 were being delivered to a provincial entity called the Alberta Junior Rugby Association. I could not comprehend how that could have occurred. Didn't players pay their dues to clubs? Didn't clubs pay their dues to regional, provincial and national organizations? How did the flow of funding redirect from the players to an organization that consisted of four or five executive volunteers, who didn't deliver the game of rugby but held all the power of the distribution of funds?

I had been the Alberta Rugby Union Managing Director when we had created a junior rugby organization to parallel the senior provincial program in providing funding to provincial teams to travel to national competitions. There had never been any intention to mess with the natural order of sport delivery in Alberta.

Similar to the first Clan executive meeting, where the age of information and technology showed me how long I had been "out of the game." I learned that it was "online" registration that had facilitated this hijacking of the regional union and clubs' rightful funding. Our best intentions of providing high-performance access to all young Albertans regardless of economic capacity had been squandered by the desire of a few politically motivated individuals. I want to clarify that I am not opposed to people having opinions contrary to mine. However, the core premise of every democratic society is the power of the will of the majority. We had a meeting. The clubs voted to regain their rightful funding. In my opinion, the Alberta Rugby Union and the Alberta Junior Rugby Association lied straight faced to all of the people present when they said, "Let us resolve this situation on your behalf." In all the years that I had been involved with rugby I had never encountered such deception, nor had I ever encountered the open vile response of the Alberta Junior Rugby Associations treasurer. I am a Canadian and being overtly rude and openly demeaning is the most offensive thing you can do. This was not the rugby environment that I had known and for the first time in all my years of preaching the rugby gospel, it occurred to me that it was time to not just move on but move out completely.[8]

Alberta Junior Girls Coaching Staff

When the universe nudges you full circle to the lessons that you thought you had already learned, you have to ask yourself, why? *Why am I experiencing the same frustrations? Why am I being triggered by even bigger injustices? Why am I so mad at this? Why am I taking this so personally? Why the hell am I even here? I have already*

---

[8] Once the 50th anniversary was completed, I was still the president of the club. The president of the club attends the both the Edmonton Rugby Union Annual General Meeting and the Alberta Rugby Union Annual General Meeting. These organizations report to their constituents, the clubs. I was in attendance of these meetings as the club's president. At this point, I had not been involved with rugby politics for a very long time. (That should lead into my experiences that finalized my decision to exit entirely.)

done and experienced and learned this? Wait a minute, I recognize you. Hiding behind the indignation of "rightness." Hello ego. Dammit! I know this stuff. How did I get so sucked in?

When I take a step back, pull out the divider between my right and left brain, let go of the judgment, let go of the "winning," let go of all the beliefs that I am no longer aligned to, it's like the "aha" of a math formula. That's simple. You are here because you need your glasses adjusted. Your perspective, looking out from those glasses has been clouded over with ego. It's like glaucoma, you don't notice yourself going blind until you can't see at all. Remember the "nanapoopoo" story? Well, here you are again. Your team, this club, is not winning. You, the "rugby guru" are going to magically make that happen. "Because you are that good!" chirps the ego voice.

Hell hath no fury like an ego-driven female coach learning her lessons twice!

"You wanna fight? Put'em up! This isn't my first rodeo!"

Whoa killer! Breathe. What happened to all your personal evolution? What happened to going with the flow? What happened to providing an environment for people, through sport, to experience what they can do, alone and with others? What happened to taking "winning" out of the equation?

Sigh. Oops. Back to square one. Oh well, at least I am recognizing it quicker now.

There were three other events that happened at this time that pointed to the possibility that this might be the impending rugby sunset in my life.

My dearest friend, Ric Suggitt, of whom I have told so many stories, died of a brain aneurism. He was so much younger than I was. How could this happen? He had just come home from the USA to Lethbridge to settle down at the University of Lethbridge and raise his kids and coast into old age. "Just relax," he told me. "Just enjoy yourself and have fun Helen, life is too short." And then he was gone.

Gareth Jones, who had been instrumental in hiring me as the executive director of the Alberta Rugby Union all those years ago, was stricken with "a little prostrate thing." And then he was gone.

The two of them were the yin and yang of my rugby career. They could barely tolerate each other. Ric thought that Gareth was an old school, pompous, jerk and Gareth thought that Ric was an undisciplined, impolite, disrespectful vagabond. They were both correct.

Gareth had descended from the Welsh valleys to Canada on a club rugby tour, where he was the coach. To Gareth, Alberta was the land of opportunity for both his professional and rugby career. He had been a young man at the end of WWII and brought with him a deep-rooted respect for the military and adherence to authority. He was Welsh and he carried the music DNA close to his love of performance. More than anything else, Gareth loved pomp and circumstance. He sincerely believed that anything he set his mind to was not just a possibility, it was an inevitability. His total confidence in his own ability to "deliver," his faith in his close supporters to "come through" and his ultimate belief that everything he dreamed had full divine backing, allowed him to create the most wonderful facilities, events, and contributions to the people around him.

The finest moments of his rugby career were those involving grand and impossible dreams: The creation of the St. Albert Rugby Club as was according to Gareth, the "finest rugby facility in Canada;" the Alberta Centenary involving three levels of high-performance games where Canada played Scotland, England U23's played Alberta, and Sanyo RFC from Japan played Edmonton. What a glorious day, full of pomp and tradition, Edmonton summer sunshine, capped with a Sanyo sponsored open bar! He trumped that off with the last hosting of the Asian Pacific Conference in Calgary and the last tour to Britain for the Alberta Senior Men's team. Since the time of "Gareth," there have been no more Asian Pacific conferences and there have been few if any international tours for any Alberta players at all. He was a dreamer and a doer and he lived his life with the same full passion that he infused into everything he did.

Though Gareth loved being front and center, there was a component of himself that he rarely shared with others. In Gareth's life there was nothing that ever preempted his family or his faith. They were the core of his existence and the purpose to his life. Though he carried an incredible passion for rugby, it was never the primary reason for his existence. Later in his life, his wife, children and grandchildren would continue to be the source of his happiness. The arrival of a great-grandchild made his military chest puff like plumage and expanded that Tom Jones smile to ignite his entire face in joy.

Through many of the political rugby revolutions and coups and the various phases of "what we really need to do now is," it was Gareth's advice that held the most value.[9]

"You can't take this stuff personally," he would say. "You have to understand that everyone who comes forward with another idea and fights against our ideas, wants the same things we do. They believe as fervently in their vision as we do in ours. You have to give them the respect that you would like them to give you, and if they don't, then you show them what that respect looks like, so they can choose differently next time."

"Helen, Helen, Helen…the most important thing is that we do the best we can with what we have, enjoy a good cigar and a nice glass of Drambuie, and then we go home to the things that truly matter to us."

As I left Gareth's funeral, I thought that he would have been pleased with all the flags and marching, with the Welsh national anthem and the music, with the huge attendance from both the St. Albert and rugby communities. I thought about how his family loved him, so I thought about all the lessons he had taught me. *Dream big; do the work; be accountable; be respectful; don't take things personally; nobody dies if we screw up rugby; and most importantly, remember what is really important: Your family and you.*

---

[9] Throughout rugby history in this country, there have been many political "over throws." At each and every time that new group comes into power, we, the membership, are always told… "What we need to do now is…"

There is never room on the stage for two bold protagonists at the same time, saying the same lines, and simply wearing different costumes. That was the situation with Ric and Gareth. They were both cut from the same cloth, but the clothes were simply different styles.

Ric Suggitt wandered into my Alberta Rugby Union office in the early '90s and told me that he thought he might like to coach rugby and that I should hire him for the youth development officer position. "Have you ever coached rugby?" I asked.

"Nah!" he replied.

"Have you ever coached anything?" I asked.

"Nah!" he replied.

"And you want me to hire you to go out and teach rugby to the masses?"

"Oh yeah!"

"OK, let's get started!"

That was the beginning of an incredible journey with an incredible man. I would book him into the cheapest hotels on the most remote locations in northern Alberta and he would never complain. He just laughed. There were occasions where he would call me and ask, "Is there really a school in Rycroft? All I can see is a gas station!" Or, "Helen, have you ever been to the Peter Pond hotel in Fort MacMurray? No, why? Is it nice?" And, "No, no Helen, it is not nice, but me and the rest of the derelicts are getting along just fine!"

Thankfully, the Fort Mac boys moved him into their own homes.[10] And that was his mission; to bring rugby to the masses. We would laugh and agree that all we needed was three gospel singers, and a tent, and we could take this show on the road!

One of my favorite Ric "Sluggo" stories (referred to earlier) is when Cheryl Dawes had him come out to Spruce Grove to her school. There was a little down Syndrome guy in the PE class, who desperately wanted to play all the fun games that Ric was teaching. At first, he took this little guy's hand and pulled him around, but when those little legs couldn't keep up, he scooped him up on his shoulders and the two of them careened and stumbled around the field tagging the rest of the kids. His little buddy was holding onto Sluggo's head for dear life and screaming with delight with every tag. Cheryl called to tell me that it was possibly the best lesson of inclusion that she had ever seen.

During Sluggo's employment with the Alberta Rugby Union there were great calls and there were not so great calls! The same guy who would light up the rugby magic with kids and teachers would also threaten to punch out a senior rugby citizen. You either loved him or hated him. If you knew him at all, there really was no middle ground. He had these values he lived by and the world was pretty simple. You either aligned to the values or you "could go fuck yourself."

The first thing you had to be was authentic. He absolutely had no time for "posers." If you were the

---

[10] Fort MacMurray has a rugby team and the reference is to those players.

wackiest player on the planet, you were safe with Ric, because there weren't too many people who could beat him in that department. There are a lot of people who spend a lot of money trying to find their "child self"—inner child. Well, I can tell you that Ric Suggitt was never more than six inches away from his eight-year-old self and that made him absolutely endearing to players and coaches alike, and generally a huge source of frustration to administrators.

You had to be hard-working and committed. He could accept your inability to do something, but he would not tolerate anyone that didn't try. If you weren't prepared to go to the bottom of the ruck (a big dog pile of tackled rugby bodies) with and for your team, it wouldn't be long before your courage would be questioned.

If Ric Suggitt was going to be your coach or friend or colleague, you better have a sense of humor and you better not take yourself too seriously because there was always a "poke" coming. Laughing was his most favorite thing in the world and there were many times when it was at the expense of someone else. I remember coaching the Pandas when Ric told everyone and mostly me that it was a good thing that I was a hooker because "those pancake hands couldn't catch a cold!" Being able to laugh at yourself takes the ego out of living. The only people who ever had a problem with Ric were those whose ego couldn't handle his honesty or his humor. The man operated without an ego. That let him move forward into any situation without any fear. It also let him connect to people in the most honest, authentic, and meaningful way. He had no shoes when he started and he had no shoes at the height of his coaching career. His success had absolutely no bearing on who he was. To all of us that made him even more loveable, but to people who operate from ego, it made him impossible to manipulate, which drove them crazy.

Pandas Coaching staff: Ric Suggitt, Matt Parrish, Maxi Miciak, Helen Wright, Kerry Yeo.

I was looking on the Clan clubhouse wall the other day, looking for the pictures of the '90s when he coached Kirby and Danny and crew and I saw the picture of the tie-dye jerseys! I laughed, *That is so Sluggo! Let's take tradition and all that old shit and just punch it in the face! "Fuckem!"*

Because he was so creative and impulsive, change was his method of operation. If you couldn't adapt, you may as well hang up those cleats. What was on the game plan yesterday could easily be totally different today, depending on how long he spent on the toilet.[11] His wife, Jenn is most

---

[11] Yes, Ric used to create plays and practices on the toilet.

conversant on Sluggo's winds of change as he followed his career from one side of this continent to the other and back.

I remember when Ric decided that he wanted a partner and that partner was going to be Jenn. He followed her everywhere, even out to the West Coast when she was managing the junior women's team and used the same approach he used for everything. "Come on, you know you want to," followed with a huge dog eating shit grin. Once Jenn came into his life, he settled right down. *Not!* She just became part of the package and everyone who has ever worked with Ric was very, very grateful. At least we could get ahold of him now.

Ric struggled with the decision to move from the senior national women's team to the senior national men's team. He was so committed to women's rugby and the honesty and commitment of that population, that moving to the bullshit of the men's national team was daunting. When we were finished drinking, yakking, and debating, he concluded that the only way you can change anything is to step right into the middle of it. And so, he did. Between him and his West Coast buddies of John Tate and Doug Tait and Rick Farrely and the others, I can't remember, he built a rugby sevens[12] program that is still climbing and left the men's rugby fifteens' program better than he found it. Where do you go when you reach the top? To the next country! Just keep moving forward! The man achieved all

---

[12] This is the name of a type of rugby game—as opposed to fifteens rugby it is sevens rugby. Implication is the number of players on the field.

of his goals and then came right to start again on the front line.

The first Rugby Canada U19/23 Women's team

We can all take a lesson from Ric! Don't be afraid, do what you want to do, do what you love to do! Have fun! Don't leave anything undone! Be who you are! Who you really are! And if anyone doesn't like it…fuckem!

I was reluctant to include the third event that happened to me, leading me to question my relationship with the game of rugby. I struggled with the old ego demon. Did I want to include this piece, given that it appeared so ego connected? But was it ego connected? Have we aligned ourselves and agreed to values that simply don't serve us anymore? Is this about my ego? I knew that I had not spent a lifetime of creating and delivering this game simply to receive accolades for doing so. I knew in my soul that my desire to help people find themselves, using this rugby medium was authentic. So, why was I so deeply hurt?

The original 1988 national women's team was invited to the West Coast during a national sevens event to be acknowledged publicly on the field in front of all the fans. I didn't even know that everyone was going. And for what? Until I saw the posting on Facebook. I wondered if in my lack of computer and social media skills, meant that I had somehow missed sending my alumni information. I contacted the Rugby Canada individual and asked if they had received my information and why I hadn't been invited to this event, given that I was on the team. She replied that even though I was standing there in the picture, had my jersey mounted on my wall, trained with the team, played in the unofficial games, I did not get onto the field that particular day and therefore was not 'capped' and therefore not part of the official team.[13] I was stunned. Every single 'not good enough' feeling from the time I was born until this moment flooded into my heart and spilled out my eyes.

In any other team sport that I have been involved with, the supporting role of the 'bench player' has been touted as vital. Professional teams without this 'depth' rarely achieve their goals. It is the premise of the entire team philosophy. When a team manager lists the 25 players for the game, they don't indicate the official players because on any given day, any one of those 25 players could impact the outcome of the game. That is why players are now being identified as

---

[13] In the early days of the game of rugby, school boys would receive a school cap for representing their school. That tradition carried onto national teams.

"strategic substitutions" or "impact players." But in 1988, in the only international game that would be available to me as a player, I did not exist. I was a ghost in the picture and that is the rule. And as I felt Ric Suggitt slide his arm around my sobbing shoulders, he whispered in my ear, "Let it go, Helen. Just let the tears flow and let it go."

I know that there is no one to blame. I know there has been no wrong doing. It is simply my perception of an organization that doesn't value me. It hurts. It makes me cry. But it is a false perception based on an old "not good enough" belief that I am releasing now, after all these years. Like the Clan boys told me, when I relayed this story to them, "Not only do we value you, we love you!"

I have two children. They are the yin and yang of my existence. Sean and I have the same passion buttons and a great love for sport and what it can provide to the human experience. My daughter, Amanda, is my grounding rod. She carries my "home" frequency. When everything seems emotionally chaotic and confusing, she provides that lovely linear logical perspective that has comforted me through many dramas and traumas. "Mom, if you are feeling a resistance or a universal push back, maybe it's time for a pause? Or a fork in the road?" What a wise woman she is.

This game and my relationship with it have provided the canvas for me to paint who I am in this world. Who I am is not what anyone says I am or am not. Only I have the authority to choose who I will be today. Who I am is not the collection of my achievements or failures. Those were only the curriculum for my learning. Who I am is not the result of my experiences or anything that happened to me. Those were simply the opportunities presented for my growth as a human. At the end of the learning circle, even with several rotations in my case, who I am is that little piece of light and joy, running barefoot across the dew-soaked clover, getting ready to fly.

The End